Ex Dono Auctoris
[olim commendalis] 4/96

MAGDALEN COLLEGE LIBRARY

SHELF No. 320,01
LEO

KV-087-130

304011321C

Modernity

WITHDRAWN

MAGDALEN COLLEGE LIBRARY

John Leonard

951323

© **John Leonard, 1996**
No part of this publication may be reproduced in any form without the permission of the author, except for short extracts in reviews or academic works.

published by the author:
John Leonard MA, PhD,
PO Box 243,
Woden, ACT 2606,
AUSTRALIA

Designed and typeset in Book Antiqua 10 on 12.5 body text by the author.
Printed and bound by CPN Publications PTY, PO Box 779, Fyshwick, ACT 2609.
The stock used in this book is low-acid archive paper.

National Library of Australia Cataloguing-in-Publication entry:

Leonard, John, 1965-.
  Modernity.

  Bibliography.
  Includes Index.
  ISBN 0 646 27616 6.

  1. Capitalism—Moral and ethical aspects. 2. Humanism.
  3. Political science—Philosophy. 4. Economic development—
  Environmental aspects. I. Title.

330.122

Contents

Foreword

The present work is offered to interested readers by the author at his own expense so that its unfamiliar argument may become less unfamiliar.

Although the work was offered to several UK and Australian publishers during 1995, none took it up. There are, I think, two reasons for this. The first is that the argument is an unfamiliar and difficult one, or rather the argument itself is not difficult, but that it is difficult to see why long-established and comfortable modes of thought need be changed for such uncomfortable and unfamiliar ones. This I hope I have explained in the following pages, though obviously not to the satisfaction of the various publishers' readers.

The second reason is that this work does not fit comfortably into any one academic discipline, and thus has no guaranteed market anywhere. However, nothing fits very neatly into the mould of any one academic discipline, and books which have a guaranteed market have a guarantee of an uncritical readership, which is the last thing I would wish for this book.

It follows that as this book has no regular publisher, then it has not gone through the process of editing which most books go through. I hope the reader will make allowances for this if confronted with a perceived lack of organisation and polish in the work.

The reader may be interested to know that a poetry sequence by the author dealing with many of ideas in this work is shortly to be published by Hale and Iremonger (Sydney), under the title of *100 Elegies for Modernity*.

This work is dedicated to my two sons, Sylvius and Oliver, as representatives of the next generation.

The ideas which are here expressed so laboriously are extremely simple and should be obvious. The difficulty lies, not in the new ideas, but in escaping from the old ones, which ramify for those brought up as most of us have been, into every corner of our minds.

J.M.Keynes, Preface to *The General Theory of Employment, Interest and Money*

What we are supplying is really remarks on the natural history of human beings; we are not contributing curiosities however, but observations which no one has doubted, but which have escaped remark only because they are always before our eyes.

Ludwig Wittgenstein, *Philosophical Investigations* §415

The Milesians
Aren't fools—it's just that they do foolish things.

Demodocus (6th Century BCE)

Introduction

The purpose of this book is threefold: firstly to give a useful, short account of the characteristics and modes of operation of modernity, that is, the era of capitalist economic development in which we currently live; secondly to provide an argument as to why modernity and modernistic social, economic and political arrangements deserve to meet with a sustained opposition seeking to modify or overturn them, (however I also provide arguments as to why traditional opposition to modernity has been largely ineffectual, insofar as this opposition springs entirely from modernity's own scheme of values), finally to sketch out what a political movement seeking to modify modernity might look like, or attempt to do. This last objective is the most tentative of the three.

This work differs from most accounts of modernity in that it is an *anti-humanistic* account. This means that it rejects the (modernistic) notion that our present western society is the best vehicle for the development of the human spirit and the resolution of perennial human problems. An anti-humanist perspective notes that human history has shown many differing cultures, each of which has organised experience and knowledge in different ways. It follows from this that there is no one goal of human development, but the notion of human development finds a different practical expression in the social practices of each culture. The notion of human development as we understand it is entirely a product of our own culture and meaningless outside it. Thus this account is, in the terminology of Wittgenstein, a 'description' (an account, insofar as it is possible, which avoids the values and terms of the system it describes) as opposed to an 'interpretation' (one which uses the scheme of values of the paradigm in question).

This emphasis means that a general moral critique of modernity along Marxist or liberal lines is much more difficult, because there is nowhere any blue-print for an ideal society laying down that societies must follow some sort of pre-existing moral code, instead moral values are entirely culturally produced. In fact the only

1

goal which can be usefully laid down for any culture would seem to be that of ensuring its own reproduction. Thus any moral critique of modernity can only be an internal, local one, and cannot challenge modernity's practice of *Realpolitik*.

However I go on to argue that, uniquely amongst the world's cultures, modernity deserves a general critique because it is ecological unsustainable on a global, not merely a local, scale. In 200 years modernity has wreaked more ecological destruction than the previous 100,000 years of human existence; resources are rapidly becoming depleted and it is difficult to see how modernity can reproduce itself beyond the next two or three generations.

Moreover it is a peculiar characteristic of modernity that its expansive and colonising impulse means that not only does it use up its own resources and fail to keep an adequate ecological 'safety-net' for its activities, but it ensures that no other culture possesses these safeguards either. By revolutionising or destroying the temporalities of other cultures modernity makes sure that it is the dominant global culture and that the exercise of any alternative policies is made next to impossible. In other words it endangers the cultural diversity of the world, as well as its ecological diversity.

Thus any political solution to the problems that modernity has created must begin with a global decolonisation and disengagement, which would allow the creation of various different economies in the various regions of the world; these might be better able to cope with the legacy of modernity.

There are several caveats which need to be given at this point. The first is that this book makes no claim to originality in any of its ideas; everything in this book is something which is already 'in the air'. However I do claim that the synthesis of the ideas and the chain of reasoning presented in the book are, to the best of my knowledge, original. I hope that this book will join the array of excellent books of 'green' political thought that have already appeared since the 1960s; if I have in the following pages differed from the mainstream of 'deep green' thought, it is only to suggest that elements within this movement are more indebted to the paradigm of modernity and modernistic thought than perhaps they might wish to be. I am convinced that only an anti-humanist perspective can make sense of modernity and allow a genuine opposition to it to emerge.

Secondly, as this is an anti-humanist account, there is nothing in it for Marxists or liberals (or at least very determined Marxists or liberals), if any such readers have got this far they had better proceed no further.

Thirdly, this book will provide no enlightenment for anyone who is not aware of, or who has chosen to ignore, the indications of ecological crisis which are obvious for anyone to see. Accounts of the ecological devastation brought about by modernity have been available any time these thirty years, and in any case it is simple common sense that it is impossible to have one's cake and eat it, a desire modernity has erected into an economic dogma—so there is no excuse for anyone's apathy, ignorance or agnosticism in this regard.

Fourthly, this book is deliberately designed to be as short and as cogent as possible. Consequently any 'skimmers' who may be reading will find that every part of it is vital to the argument and needs to be read; however, anyone who reads the first three chapters will get some sort of idea of the intellectual environment which gave rise to this book.

Fifthly, it is written in numbered paragraphs. This is an attempt to make the argument easier to follow and to make cross-referencing possible. However, anyone perplexed by this may simply ignore the numbers, as the argument flows on through each chapter anyway.

Sixthly, the method of citation: I have not followed the academic practice of giving a citation for every statement, as the resulting bibliography would be huge and useless. Instead I have left unsupported every statement of commonly accepted fact, or fact which a forgiving reader will not mind allowing for the sake of the argument. I have however cited authorities for most of the statistics and where I am indebted to another author for a particular point or argument.

Finally, terminology: where I use the term 'modernistic' I intend it to mean 'pertaining to modernity' and not 'pertaining to literary modernism', similarly 'modernisation' means 'the political or practical imposition of modernistic temporalities'. For reasons explained in §2.5 I refer to any future non-modernistic political or cultural space as 'praeter-modern'; the term 'pre-modern' has no value-judgement attached to it, either positive or negative. 'Temporality' is defined in §1.3. I should add, for the benefit of readers in the United States, that when I write of 'liberals', I am not talking only about left-leaning members of the Democratic Party, but about anyone whose philosophy is based on the Individual, Choice, Freedom &c (and on the unspoken foundations of economic growth, continuing environmental degradation and cultural and economic imperialism). In other words almost anyone within modernity, left, centre or right.

I should also add that whatever I write has two functions: to provide those sympathetic to its premises and conclusions with argument, information and amusement, and to annoy and bewilder the unsympathetic—*Modernity* is no exception.

MAGDALEN COLLEGE LIBRARY

Chapter One:
The Temporality of Modernity

1.1 The term 'modernity' is being used increasingly by cultural historians as a label to attach to the period in which we are living, and to help define its characteristics. However, there is currently little agreement as to what these characteristics actually are, when the beginnings of modernity can be located, and even whether or not modernity can be said to have come to an end. I shall be giving my own definition of modernity shortly (§§1.2, 1.3), but before doing so I should like to pause to note two interesting features of the concept 'modernity'.

The first of these is that although the term has only recently come into vogue in this sense (it is not in the *OED*), yet the fact that it has been adopted widely points to the fact that this period likes to think of itself as different from all other ages. And not only different, we might add, but somehow as the culmination of human history. This, it should be noted, is in contrast to most human societies which have usually thought of themselves as declining from some previous period of excellence or virtue. Moreover it should also be noted that very rarely have people ever given a label to the period in which they live; such labels as 'The (European) Dark Ages', 'The Renaissance', 'Pre-Columbian America' or 'The Abbassid Caliphate' are usually *post facto* and convey some measure of (usually European) judgement upon the period. Most people who have ever lived have probably not thought of themselves as living in this or that period, but in 'the present', 'now'; that is, if the question 'what do you call the age in which you are living?' would have had any meaning for them.

Furthermore it should be noted that, although the term 'modernity' is so recent, the labels that are attached to other periods of European history, which have been in general use for at least a century, namely 'The Dark Ages', 'The Middle Ages', 'The Renaissance' and 'The Enlightenment', form a series which implies some culminating epoch, such as Modernity.

The second point to make about the term 'modernity' is that its scope is not geographically restricted as are the descriptions applied to other periods, even

4

'The Enlightenment'. Thus modernity is taken to be a description which can apply to all parts of the world equally. Indeed, metaphorically 'the modern world' is seen to be all of a piece, at an uniform level of economic and technological development (even though this is not the case), and as constituting a single life-way. Thus we can conclude that the concept of 'modernity' is a comforting one for modernity's subjects in that modernity is seen in this view as both singular and signal. This study will attempt to show that modernity is indeed singular, singularly unfortunate, and signal after a fashion, though neither recognition is a cause for celebration.

1.2 My own definition of modernity is that of the economic and cultural system which began to emerge in the late eighteenth century in England as a result of the technological innovations of that century, principally in the textile and iron industries, though innovations in agriculture also played their part (Clark in Mokyr 242, 262). Some historians believe that the modern period can be said to begin with the development of urban life, banking and international trade which occurred from the late (European) Middle Ages onwards. Certainly the material and technological development of this period was a necessary cause of the Industrial Revolution, but whether this was a sufficient cause, and modernity an inevitable outcome, I doubt. For one thing many societies have reached a comparable stage of material and technological development (Ming China, for example), without ever proceeding towards a capitalistic economy. For another teleological explanations are all too easy in history; it is very comforting to imagine that everything that has ever happened in history is for the express purpose of leading up to the present moment. Indeed there is currently a fashion amongst historians to search through the past in order to confirm that everyone has always really been a proto-capitalist and that all societies have secretly come to find that the only solutions to perennial economic realities are very like the ones we have now (this is in contrast to earlier generations of historians who searched through the past in order to discover how different, and therefore inferior, everyone before modernity was). In fact, of course, the perennial economic realities that other societies have faced have, like the economic realities we face, simply been aspects of the way their societies were organised, and as their societies were not organised in the same way as ours, then the realities they faced were not ours.

I choose the Industrial Revolution as the starting point of modernity not, as with Romantic accounts of history which see the Industrial Revolution as some sort of Fall, from agricultural, organic, 'moral' societies, to industrial, inauthentic and market economies. In fact many parts of the world had been industrialised for centuries before the eighteenth century, and all cultures are, so to speak,

5

'inauthentic'; those who believe that pre-modern societies were 'moral', or some-how more moral than ours, are deluded.

Nevertheless, against the current fashion to downgrade the concept of the Industrial Revolution, it is necessary to insist that something occurred in latter half of the eighteenth century which enabled people to multiply capital in a way never seen before. Thus in the early eighteenth century the GNP of Britain was growing so that it would have doubled every 346 years; a century later it was growing so as to double once every 28 years. So clearly something happened and that not just the discovery of a series of techniques of manufacture, but the alignment of a number of social discourses, by which existence and work were structured, so that a whole new way of thinking about existence and work and of organising them, and concentrating them into the one economy, came about.

Exactly what the transformation of the economy of Britain that emergent capitalism effected was needs to be looked at more closely to distinguish it from the preceding period. It is not simply a question of technological development coupled with the 'division of labour' which Adam Smith hailed (as though labour had never been divided before). Nor is it a direct result of successive technological innovations, each one dependent on the last; although these *are* very important in the history of capitalism. What seems to be the defining characteristic of moder-nity is an economy where, when the profits of an enterprise come to be used in further investment, knowingly or unknowingly, directly or indirectly, a part of these profits comes to be invested in further innovations in production — this is what we might call *the continuous revolution in production*.

To give a more specific example of this process: a history of iron and steel production might concentrate on the various technological innovations which have taken place, from Coalbrookdale to the latest computerised steel mill. Each new innovation will, no doubt, be accompanied by a spurt of production, as more steel is produced, more plants come into operation &c &c. But this series of innovations is against a background of continually rising production, made possible, year by year, by improvements in transport, improvements in the organisation of indus-try and the workforce, by new accessions of iron ore, by increasing markets, by the greater availability of capital and so on. (One lucky accident which happened in the mid nineteenth century was the opening up of the American Mid-West to cereal growing. It could well be argued that this guaranteed the continuance of modernistic growth, and still does (§§6.4, 6.6)). Some of these are direct and explicit innovations in production, but others are the result of indirect investment — the general 'advance' or 'growth' of the capitalistic regime of production on a broad front.

1.3 Another way of expressing the thesis of §1.2 is to say that modernity has revolutionised the temporalities of human existence. A temporality is the way any particular society has of organising time and activity (in the sense used here it is a revival of an older word for regime or polity (*OED* **Temporality** 1)). It is well known, for example that until this century most people did not possess clocks or watches and did not need to. It is the transformation of society into a timekeeping one which has necessitated an individual concern for timekeeping, as Norbert Elias has argued in his *Time: An Essay*.

It should be noted that what I describe as a temporality is not a thing that has an independent existence, but something deduced from the broad range of culture practices, institutions and technologies that obtain. These practices, institutions and technologies are of course heterogeneous, polyphyletic (to adopt a botanical term), various, local and contingent cultural artefacts and in most cultures they are so diverse as to prevent one from ever saying that a particular culture has a particular purpose, ethos, *Zeitgeist*, or whatever. They are diverse in modernity too, except that some cruel god or other brought it about that all the important parts of this cultural baggage could be made to point towards economic development, and a aesthetics of personal and human development to go with it. (This is perhaps why it is only in modernity that concepts such as ethos or *Zeitgeist* are found at all). It is certainly the reason for our obsession with economic growth, which is different in kind from the interest in well-being and prosperity which every culture shows. All political thinkers in the Western tradition before modernity, for example, are interested in prosperity, but see it as a *sign* of a well-functioning society. Only modernity thinks of prosperity as a *precondition* for civilised life.

Thus it comes about that everything material in modernity points to the one end, and, for example, steam engines, the liberal subject, modern banking, the nuclear family and so on, all of which had appeared or were appearing independently of modernity, became caught up in it, and found their places as adjuncts to its development.

In fact I can now extend the point I made in §1.1 and note that if modernity thinks of itself as a unique chapter in human history, this is understandable since modernity has effected the second great transformation of temporalities in human history. The first transformation was the transition from the rhythms of a hunter/gatherer economy, with its seasonal pursuit of game animals and its seasonal exploitation of plant foods, to the equally seasonal, but very different, rhythms of the agricultural year. This transformation, although it effectively began human history by permitting the establishment of sedentary, literate societies, was not total: it had taken, by the beginnings of modernity, nearly 10,000 years and was

MAGDALEN COLLEGE LIBRARY

not by any means uniform or complete – there were still substantial populations of hunter/gatherers in the world and many societies which combined the temporalities of hunting and gathering with those of agriculture.

In the next section I shall be outlining the model of temporalities more fully. Suffice it to say here that I do not see temporalities as being altogether homogenous, with one temporality in operation at any one time and place. Instead temporalities can be thought of as piled one above the other, although older temporalities are ones which have less cultural leverage. Thus it is important to realise that the agricultural temporality was not uniform across the world, nor even uniform throughout each separate society, but instead it varied with status, gender, geographical location &c. Nor were these temporalities part of a changeless, eternal cycle. Nevertheless it is also to be noted that all the 'official' history of wars, conquests, religious change &c &c up until the beginning of modernity was played out against the relatively slow-changing background of agricultural temporalities. It can be plausibly argued, for example, that a peasant in 1700 in one of the more isolated parts of England had much the same life-style, and much of the same technology, as his Neolithic ancestor of 6,000 years earlier.

Modernity has in 200 years effected a greater transformation than the previous 10,000 years. It has, for example, turned agriculture in the developed world into an occupation pursued by a tiny fraction of the population, instead of by the majority, and seems set to do the same thing to the developing world. Another indication of this overwhelming change is that hunter/gatherer peoples have fared very badly in modern times, and only a handful of the dozens of hunter/gather societies which existed in 1800 still exist.

I shall go on to discuss how completely modernity can be said to have revolutionised the temporalities of life in a moment. But it needs to be said again that modernity's impulse seems always towards the *intensification* of productivity. Thus in place of the various economies and temporalities of the agricultural phase of human history we have the single dominant temporality of modernity and the single, capitalist world-economy it strives towards. On the level of the organisation of labour modernity transforms the seasonal cycle of killingly hard work during sowing and harvest, followed by comparative ease at other times, with a regimen of hard work year-round. It should be remembered that, onerous as the 40-hour week is, it is only the recent development of the 60, or even 80 hour weeks worked by the first generations of modernity's factory-fodder, and still worked by workers in developing countries to produce cheap consumer goods to bolster up the middle-class lifestyles of the developed world. Other palliatives such as paid holidays, sick pay and maternity leave were secured even more recently, and are even less universal.

1.4 If, as we have said, pre-modern history was played out against a background of agricultural temporalities (§1.3), then it is fair to say in contradistinction that modernity, and specifically the development of capital, in its revolutionising of these temporalities has, as it were, become history. Yet this view of modernity needs to be supplemented by a closer look at exactly how far modernity can be said to have revolutionised these prior temporalities and replaced it with its own.

For it will be apparent that although modernity is in some measure the dominant temporality, it is by no means the only one. There are, for example, many places in the world where older agricultural temporalities still obtains, or is mixed with a newer temporalities, as when Asian factory-workers work in the mornings in the factory and on their small-holdings in the afternoon. Even in societies which have been largely industrialised for several generations, such as the United States or parts of Japan, the workers do not behave in exactly the same way, even though they may participate equally in the world market.

Indeed sometimes the existence of a differing temporality in modernity can be a positive advantage to those who differ, as witness the success of migrant-Asian and Chinese in western societies in small business. Here the economics of the extended family are more efficient in such low-profit enterprises than those of the western individual. Only when businesses grow larger than the extended family can usefully participate in do the proprietors begin to find modernistic business methods better suited to their plans.

To a certain extent this lack of homogeneity is due to the society and the *a priori* conditions and characteristics which modernity found when it first effected its revolution in any particular region. But temporalities are best thought of as being superimposed, like archaeological strata, the most recent being the most effective in influencing economic and individual behaviour. Thus it is a modernistic temporality which will always the one to initiate and influence economic activity and the 'modernisation' of that activity.

Another view of this would see modernity as always engaged in new colonisation of pre-modern spaces. If the temporalities of these cultural spaces are convenient to modernity's purposes then they can persist for some time, even within otherwise completely modernised societies — one thinks, for example, of the Japanese 'outwork' system, or that country's heavily-protected rice-farming industry. It is rarely the first-world organisation which benefits which actually carries out the act of colonial plunder; it is not the US beef industry which clears Central and South American forests, but the impoverished and dispossessed peasants of the area, acting, in their eyes, in their own best interests, or perhaps under coercion.

In another view of this aspect of modernity Ivan Illich has described as 'Shadow Work' the work which, in pre-modern times, was a part of day to day activity, such as cleaning, laundry and child-care, and is now relegated to the space of so-called 'leisure-time', or that of unpaid 'housework'. And such 'shadow work', the remnants of prior temporalities, is always an important constituent of modern societies and constitutes part of the unpaid-for social structure which capitalist enterprise relies upon.

Thus it is useful to think of modernity as constantly engaged in rolling back the frontiers of pre-modern temporalities and indigenous modes of social organisation. Colonisation has often been thought of as strictly external to the core-territories of capitalism, and as being concerned with raw materials and cheap labour. This was certainly the character of early external colonialism (say to 1945), a colonialism which carried on many of the imperatives of pre-modern European colonisation of the period 1450-1800. But it is worth remembering that modernity had to carry out first a substantial (and still ongoing) *internal* colonisation of all the pre-modern spaces within European countries, and then began a second phase of external colonisation (which ironically has occurred within the so-called 'Post-Colonial' period (§2.2)). This phase is concerned, as well as with the older imperatives of raw materials and cheap labour, with the creation of new markets for goods.

For it should be noted that the creation of markets for its products is the first and last imperative of modernity. This is in contrast to modernity's own view of itself, which is that it mobilises revolutions in production to fulfil better various crying human needs. In truth these needs are strictly of its own making — as T.S.Ashton, in his classic study *The Industrial Revolution* (1948) put it, 'invention is the mother of necessity'. To give an example of internal colonisation, for example, we might cite domestic laundry, which 200 years ago was usually done in a stream with home-made soap. As modernity develops a market in this cultural space we see home-made soap replaced with factory-made soap, the stream with a hot-water copper, fired with bought coal, the copper replaced by a washing machine and the soap with detergent, and perhaps, finally, the whole process being super-seded by a wide-spread adoption of dry-cleaning.

Thus we can say that modernity is always, to use a popular phrase 'on a roll', capital is always developing on a broad front and expanding into cultural and geographical spaces never before colonised. This is why, to return to the second point of §1.1, modernity is assumed to be the temporality of the entire world even though the world is still imperfectly modernised.

1.5 The model of a modernistic temporality imposed upon prior temporalities seems to be a better description of the reality of modernistic capitalism than a cruder model of cultural domination. The latter model continues racist and elitist western colonialist attitudes by implying that all non-western people are victims, have no agency whatsoever, and are perhaps rather stupid and sheep-like. In truth of course we have to say that the temporality of later modernity is so far from being imposed upon anyone that it actually looks like and seems to be an escape from former colonising paradigms. It is moreover so extremely plausible that almost everyone in the developed world still believes that it is the best system to serve the greatest number of crying needs, even when the history of the last two hundred years shows that it is not. Thirdly, unlike cruder models of economic and political domination, it is possible to describe a modernistic temporality as a sort of tool-bag, from which those in developing countries can extract one or two items, whilst preserving aspects of their pre-modern culture. In point of fact the temporality of modernity is like phosphorus in air, and cannot help but start into fiery life as soon as it is exposed, and in the long term, to continue the metaphor, will consume everything in its way, leaving a few, unimportant, cultural differences as the markers of that liberal fetish, diversity.

A very good example of the imposition of a new temporality upon other societies is the so-called 'Green Revolution', which began in the 60s and 70s, though it has proved to be a foretaste of the 'modernisation' of the less-developed world in the 80s and 90s. (Nor has the ongoing modernisation of agriculture slackened in the least since). The outline of this movement is well-known. Faced with a growing population in the Third World, first-world plant breeders and biologists conceived the idea of applying first-world techniques of plant-breeding and agriculture to the Third World (that the best solution to the over-population caused by a partial modernisation of the economies of various Third World countries (§6.8) was the modernisation of those countries' agricultural systems was accepted without demur). Consequently various 'super-crops', particularly rice, were developed to be high yielding, and widely introduced throughout the Third World.

While it is true that the Green Revolution did allow a greater production of crops, this high-yield was bought at a price. In the first place the new super-crops were all bred to be highly-resistant, not to disease, but to weed-killing chemicals and insecticides, and highly responsive to chemical fertilisers. Was it any coincidence that the multi-national companies most involved with the development of these new varieties were also those most involved with the sale and distribution of chemical fertilisers, weed-killers and insecticides? Certainly the most obvious effect of the Green Revolution has been to destroy traditional and locally-suitable varieties of crops (§7.2) and to take seed-merchanting out of local hands.

MAGDALEN COLLEGE LIBRARY

Another problem has been the disruption of the ecological habitats of traditional farming. Previously the local bird, fish and amphibian fauna had proved useful for insect-control, but with the new regime of chemical insecticides they rapidly disappeared. The case of the south-east Asian farmers whose yield increased manyfold but who were still worse-off, because the fish which used to live in their paddy-fields, and which they use to eat, had disappeared, is well-known. It has also been the case that many of the new varieties proved to be very susceptible to disease, and instead of a situation of low, but predictable, yield many areas found themselves in a situation where a high yield one year was succeeded by a catastrophic harvest-failure the next.

But the least recognised, but most profound, effect of the Green Revolution has been to bring Third World agriculture into the world economic system. Although the way that the new agriculture was organised and implemented varied from country to country typically the Green Revolution saw the dispossession of the smaller land-owners and farmers, who could not afford the new crop varieties, or whose fields were too small and inefficient for mechanised harvesting, or who were less well integrated into government bureaucracy, in favour of larger land-owners. The dispossessed peasantry then headed to the already over-crowded towns and added to the population problem. Thus the Green Revolution, we can say is a temporality imposed on older temporalities, which had the effect of, as it were, introducing agriculture, and often agriculture for export and trading, not just local needs, where previously there had been simply living.

1.6 There are two final points which need to made in this opening chapter. The first is to re-emphasise that modernity is a dynamic, revolutionary process, how-ever it may hide behind social conservatism. It is continually engaged in cutting away at the edges of other temporalities, and colonising new cultural and geographical spaces. This is hardly surprising since it is much easier to create a market for new products, or to revolutionise a older method of production, than it is to succeed in an already-established market. (This argument, though not its terminology or application, is basically the same as Joseph Schumpeter's well-known economic explanation for modernity's strong imperative of innovation). It is this reason also why the competition of the market-place usually produces unstable monopolies and informal cartels in well-established markets, rather than the dynamic competitive environment it is supposed to.

The consideration that modernity is a 'frontier-mentality' also invites specula-tion as to what will happen when there are no more frontiers. This is something I will be considering in the latter half of the book (§6.1 *et seq*).

But finally, and as a way of leading into the next chapter, I should like to make the point that dynamism and activity are often valued for their own sakes in modernity. As I shall be arguing later in the book much of modern 'development' is not only useless, but ecological imprudent, not to say insane. One thinks of the enormous stocks of weapons of all descriptions stockpiled in various parts of the world. On a more mundane level it is obvious that the First World is vastly over-resourced, for example it is by no means obvious why every suburban house in the West needs a lawn-mower, when one for every twenty houses would do just as well, to say nothing of why suburban houses need lawns anyway. It needs saying again and again that so-called economic efficiency is not some description of reality that all must heed at their peril, but simply one of the *culturally produced* markers of modernistic economics, which, however, as things are currently organised, all must still heed at their peril.

It should also be noted that modernity is solidly based upon economic growth, and not only must this growth be positive (as it was even in the very depths of the Great Depression), but it cannot, by the Accelerator Principle of economics, even slacken in its acceleration, lest a down-turn ensue. The best illustration of this is the deference paid to the figures of Gross Domestic Product (which always have to be seen to be rising). The GDP, as has been pointed out by a many a Green economist (eg Jacobs 54) is no measure of anything tangible like, Useful Work Done, or Genuine Happiness Achieved (indeed how could these be defined or measured in terms that could be universally agreed?) but simply of the growth of an economy, a very easily calculated figure. However it cannot measure the exploitation of the unpaid-for use value of the natural environment, or properly exclude the expenditure on measures to repair ecological damage. Thus the degradation of resources is 'good business' and leads to an increase in GDP. Various other figures such as NEW (Net Economic Welfare) do attempt to exclude the profits of things which, like the repair of ecological damage, should logically not be included. Yet there is no agreement as to how well these figures measure welfare, and, not surprisingly, the various published figures of NEW also all increase steadily in modernity, which increases one's suspicion of them.

Chapter Two:
A Very Brief History of Capital

There are two reasons for subjoining at this point a very brief history of capital. The first is to give some sort of historical location for the very generalised description of the workings of modernity attempted in chapter one. However the second is to describe the way in which certain characteristics of capitalistic modernisation remain constant throughout the two hundred years of modernity, and this will be apparent in my descriptions of the three phases into which it is be convenient to divide capitalism. I should say that in the main lines of my description in this chapter I am following the accounts of Michel Beaud and Martyn Lee, amongst others.

2.1 The first phase of capitalism is the longest, but also the simplest to describe; this the *laissez faire* phase which began with the beginnings of capitalism itself and lasted until the Second World War. Early capitalism is characterised by the uneven expansion of a capitalist temporality into the pre-modern economies of the core-territories of modernity. By the end of the period many European nations and the United States were approaching full industrialisation and many other territories were beginning to develop in this way.

However we should also remember that the Industrial Revolution also brought about the *de-industrialisation* of many areas of the world. In Britain, for example, East Anglia, industrialised for centuries, lost its industries in one generation and became an exclusively agricultural province. More unfortunately Ireland lost most of its traditional industries in the late eighteenth century to competition with the newly-mechanised industries of Britain coupled with discriminatory British government regulation, and was further impoverished; a similar thing happened to the Indian cotton industry in the nineteenth century. As modernity expands its sphere the same story can be told again and again.

Although the period of the late nineteenth century is usually regarded as the high point of European expansion and imperialism, the external colonisation of the period is better regarded as what Weber described as the 'capitalistic adventurer's' sort of colonisation (20) — one which pays more regard to the delimination of spheres of influence and the securing of plunder than the systematic modernisation of colonised territories. However the social and legal 'reforms' attempted out by the British administration in India, to give only one example, point the way to later developments. The 'settler' colonies of the USA, Canada, Australia &c were also consolidated during this period, thus securing, as it has turned out, a secondary expansion of the core-territories of modernity.

The theoretical ideal of this period of capitalism was an aggressive individualistic liberalism, and coupled with this, the demand for Free Trade. Free Trade was generally achieved, but only when convenient for the participatory states. Britain, having benefited from Free Trade in the period 1842-70, before any other competitors caught up with it, quixotically persisted with Free Trade when it was at a disadvantage, until the 1932 Ottawa Conference, when 'Commonwealth Free Trade' was introduced.

This period was punctuated by a series of economic crises, culminating in that of the Great Depression of 1929-1933 and beyond. Some have argued that these were caused by periodic crises in production: this is when too many goods are produced for the market and, when workers are laid off and businesses go bankrupt, confidence collapses and a general depression of trade and production results. Certainly this is a plausible interpretation, but there are others. I would only want to say here that the *fact* of these periodic crises, whatever their cause, shows the uneven and unstable nature of capital development. (In the same way we can say that *fact* that economists can disagree about the workings of the global market and appropriate national economic policy, rather than the truth of any one of their particular theoretical models, shows that they are dealing with something so complex and dynamic that no explanation will explain it, or have sufficient predictive power to deal with it).

2.2 The beginnings of Middle Capitalism are not precisely locatable insofar as, although the period can be said to begin after the Second World War, many of its components can be seen in operation much earlier.

The second period of capitalism's distinguishing feature is an *intensification* of production, the initial task of industrialisation having been accomplished. One of the earliest examples of this is the work of Frederick W.Taylor in American industry. Taylor was the founder of the twentieth-century movement which seeks to make industrial and other processes more efficient by the use of time-and-motion studies. Taylor, who began his working life in the factory, as a worker and then a foreman, began his career as a consultant by trying to eliminate workers' attempts to control the tempo of their work. He had found that workers who were paid piece-rates did not work as fast as possible to produce the maximum number of units of whatever, since they had found that the more efficient they were the less they were paid per unit. Consequently there had arisen a widespread practice, known as 'soldiering', where workers agreed amongst themselves to work more slowly in order to keep piece-rates up, and to secure for themselves a more tolerable rate of work, which also allowed them to preserve a certain pride in their work. Taylor by contrast, recommended payment by the hour but with rigidly enforced production quotas (Beaud 127-28). (It is an interesting example of double standards that Tayloristic measures employed to increase production in the Soviet coal industry in 1930s (using the rate of production of expert coal-cutter Stakhanov as a standard applied to all miners) have always been decried as Stalinist tyranny of the very worst order, but, at the same time, Taylor has been celebrated as a hero of modernisation for his work in American factories).

In 1914 Henry Ford, who enforced Tayloristic work-practices in his factories, found a remedy to the chronic absenteeism which was the workers' response to his measures; he began to pay workers the then unheard of wage of $5 for a 8-9 hour day. This was raised successively in the years after the First World War to keep it ahead of standard wages and Ford's example became the model for the adoption of similar policies in many other industries in the USA (Beaud 156-57). The, probably quite accidental, consequence of this shift in industrial policy was the beginning of the modern mass-consumption society. Since workers were both dedicated to a regular work-cycle (higher wages were only granted to 'steady' workers) and had cash in hand, the new resources of the skilled working-class were now channelled into the domestic and leisure spheres. Henry Ford himself was not the least beneficiary of his own policies, as the symbol of the new mass market became the Model T Ford, now within the price-range of skilled workers.

However, it was another thirty years before the mass market in the United States was able to influence other parts of the capitalist world and even the United States was not immune to the effects of world-wide recession after 1929. During this slump John Maynard Keynes published his *General Theory of Employment, Money and Interest* (1935) in which he argued, to reduce his argument to a sentence, that supply does not create markets automatically. In other words that the problem with capitalism is that it is subject to periodic crises in confidence, whereas, as he would never have put it, if everyone kept their nerve and pretended that nothing was wrong, then investment, and therefore economic activity, could continue unabated. Failing this, Keynes argued, it is the government's duty to continue investment and to maintain full employment, if necessary, in his words, by employing people to dig holes and fill them in again. The point being that any investment has the effect of keeping money circulating and keeping businesses in business. This was the basis of the US 'New Deal' of the 1930s. After the Second World War quasi-Keynesian policies were adopted by many governments in industrialised countries with the intention of maintaining employment at consistently higher levels than had been possible in early capitalism, when employment had boomed and crashed with the economy. An important constituent of this was the Welfare State, versions of which were institutionalised in various countries. This economic regime was institutionalised internationally with the setting up, at the Bretton Woods Conference in 1944 (at which Keynes played a leading role), of the International Monetary Fund, the World Bank and the apparatus of fixed exchange rates. This had the effect of reintroducing, in a more flexible form, the pre-war gold-standard, based on the US dollar, and, by postponing or moderating crises, of producing the most sustained period of single-minded economic growth in world history. Even already industrialised countries managed growth of up to 6% per annum (in early capitalism the annual growth rate was usually 2-3%) and this was also the era of the emergence of the new Asian economies, the first in seniority being that of Japan.

Keynes himself had predicted that only a certain amount of economic growth was necessary before people forget about further growth and could set about enjoying life (§3.2). But in the mad growth after the Second World War all thought of this was lost—economic growth had become an end in itself with the creation of ever greater needs to fulfil; as Fordism was widely adopted by employers so the 'Consumer Society' was born.

Moreover as a result of the corner-cutting necessary to reduce the manufacturing costs of items of mass consumption, or as a matter of deliberate policy, most consumer goods which resulted from this social change were (and are) very badly made. Their 'built in obsolescence', and the fact that they were not designed to be repaired, encouraged the habit of repeated purchases of the same item every few years. The emergence of mass advertising, and the application of the previously upper-class notion of fashion to consumer-goods, also stimulated the habit. Advertising had the further effect of stimulating demand for, for example, smaller items of food or domestic cleaning products. Previously many of these items had been home-made (bread, cakes, jam, biscuits &c) or one simple item had been used for many tasks (eg soap for washing, laundry, cleaning the floor, replaced by cosmetic soap, detergent, floor-cleaner &c). Thus a further colonisation of pre-modern cultural spaces resulted.

We should note that the spending which Keynes had envisaged on the social infrastructure of various countries (schools, hospitals &c), although impressive,

MAGDALEN COLLEGE LIBRARY

was overshadowed by increased profits from industry, increasing concentration of economic activity in large national or international enterprises, with the disappearance of many smaller, local businesses, increasing disruption of traditional societies and ecological damage, and the increasing stockpile of weapons, conventional, nuclear and chemical, which many countries built up by excessive spending in the 'defence' sector of their economies (Robinson 22).

A final point to make in this section is to note that sometime and somehow in Middle Capitalism the idea was firmly cemented in popular consciousness that the capitalist way of life and the economic and political arrangements necessary for its continuance are somehow connected with democracy, and that this lifeway is the only possible way of life for any human. European culture has long suffered from a superiority complex, so one element of this belief is readily explainable. It is difficult to account precisely for the idea that capitalism is democracy, or a democratic way of life. Perhaps the 'freedom' of the market is thought of as the mark of an act of Hegelian self-determination (as though we choose the way we live any more than any other society's members do (cf §3.1)). Another reason for the equation may be the immense prestige reaped after the Second World War by the Allies (forgetting Russia, which had borne the brunt of the war-effort against Germany), which was then deliberately played upon by the western propaganda machine during the Cold War.

Whatever the reason for this belief, suffice it to say that democracy, or more properly democratic procedures in the widest sense, are not the prerogative of modernity. Nor are the democratic procedures which are found in modernity of much use in moderating the excesses of modernity. The only change which I can detect within modernity which was brought about by democracy is the election of various socialist or left-of-centre governments in many European and other developed states in the 1920s, 30s and 40s (Roosevelt's Democratic administration in the US would come under this heading). These governments shifted, to a lesser or greater extent the balance of power away from the upper and upper-middle classes, to the mass middle-class of Middle Capitalism (although of course this is ultimately, despite 'profligate socialist welfare spending' not detrimental to the interests of the said upper and upper-middle classes). Moreover, this transition may well have happened anyway, without any democratic intervention. Finally we should note that democracy has been little help in curbing the social cruelty of late capitalist policies of the 70s and 80s (§2.4).

2.3 Late Capitalism had its origin in the oil-price rises of the early 1970s, although signs of a strain in the world economic order had been visible for some years before this. In fact the Oil Crisis of the early 70s simply confirmed the view amongst economists and leaders of business and government that capitalism could not bear redistributional policies, no matter how modest, in the long term. (It is worth remembering that, regardless of what capitalism might be capable of, if stretched, what really determines what it can do are those who influence international investment: economists, advisers, directors and so forth, and their social-consciences are not as well-developed as those of liberal social-planners).

It should also be remembered that the characteristics of Late Capitalism, although they represent a sharp break with the period of quasi-Keynesian policy of the 50s and 60s, carry on many of the characteristics of that period, most notably the modernisation and technological development of industry, and the concentration of economic activity in large national and international enterprises; in other words, once again, the *intensification* of economic activity.

However Late Capitalism can also plausibly be seen as a simple-minded return to the dogmas of Early Capitalism, particularly its fetishisation of Free Trade, its emphasis on private enterprise and 'deregulation' and its lack of concern for the maintenance of full employment.

For the most obvious feature of Late Capitalism is the extent to which the unskilled workers and their dependents, the bottom 10-25% of society (that is the 2-5% who were still unemployed even in the 50s and 60s, added to the 8-12% unemployment rate which has persisted in most industrial countries in the 80s and 90s, plus 'non-people', the young, the old, the mentally ill, the homeless, travellers, and other groups who are simply invisible to societal scrutiny). Although Middle Capitalism had done little for this group of people, it was more than any other period of modernity. For they, almost as soon as Late Capitalism started, were suddenly abandoned by deregulative governments, particularly in the United States and in Britain, and left to their own efforts.

The high unemployment levels of Late Capitalism are created and at times made worse, though they are never made very much better, by the troughs and crests of economic depressions and recoveries, the reappearance of periodic 'boom and bust' cycles, now affecting the entire world-economy. Thus the economic 'recovery' of the late 70s was succeeded by the slump of the early 80s; the 'recovery' of the mid 80s was in turn superseded by slump conditions beginning with the British Stock Market Crash of October 1987 and similar 'crashes' elsewhere. At the time of writing (1995) another 'recovery' is under way, but there is nothing to indicate that another slump is not going to occur in two or three years' time; nor have I heard any explanation, from economists or commentators, as to why it should not occur.

It is tempting to blame this instability on a particular cause ('the pain of modernisation', the length of time it takes the economy to recover its natural

MAGDALEN COLLEGE LIBRARY

equilibrium after the 'profligate socialist spending' of the 60s) or on individuals (for example the traders of the international currency market, whose daily trading turnover exceeds the *annual* turnover of most national economies). Indeed what makes reading newspapers and watching the television news so hilarious at this particular time of up-swing is that so much positively moral emphasis is placed upon the obtaining the right *kind* of growth. For we must not have any old growth that sucks in imports and sees a failure to renew investment. Since governments, however, in these deregulated times, will not legislate to curb imports or to encourage investment, the resulting exhortations point to a sort of personal aesthetics of growth, with an emphasis on the right kind, and not the false, hollow semblance of growth. The likeness of these tropes to those of Romantic aesthetics is remarkable, and not surprising, since they emerge from the same discursive locus.

In truth, however, it is capitalism which is unstable and the fact that most commentators now writing grew up during a period when, as result of complex and costly policies, the world-economy was temporarily stabilised, probably explains the nostalgia for a regulated world-economy on the left, or, on the other side of politics, the belief that markets can ever reach equilibrium. (The notion that unregulated markets can ever distribute goods or incomes either wisely or equitably must be corrected by the observation that even the simplest and smallest market conceivable cannot do this (Robinson 209-11)).

Late capitalism also continues the intensification of economic growth by the familiar means of internal and external colonisation. Externally the 1980s were characterised by a cruel depression in commodity prices and an equally cruel calling in of debt which, policed by the IMF, reduced many 'developing nations' to poverty once again. Yet at the same time external colonialism reached its most definitive form so far when first-world interest in third-world nations began to shift from the extraction of raw material and cheap labour to the extraction of raw materials, cheap labour *and* the expansion of western marketing into colonised countries. For the most pressing need of industry is always to expand markets (Robinson 165).

Internally and externally the 1980s and 90s have seen advertising and marketing of goods, and particularly *services,* reach new levels of frenzy. Products, gadgets and services have now been invented that would have baffled designers even in the 1960s. Services such as tourism, food, entertainment and information have the great advantage that their products are rarely durable and are therefore purchased repeatedly, to the advantage of the provider.

2.4 At this point it would be useful to mention the idea of the 'postmodern', the critical notion that somehow modernity is at an end, or has turned into something else. 'Postmodern' first arose as the name of that style of architecture which, in the late 60s and early 70s, set itself up against the prevailing 'modern' architecture of quasi-Keynesian societies (concrete, functional &c). Postmodern buildings were self-consciously eccentric, mixing styles in an eclectic no-style which was designed to emphasise the 'fun' of deliberately foiling expectation, of using traditional features in a non-traditional, or non-functional way. Later the term came to be employed to describe a particular sort of advertising, which cleverly failed to mention the product being advertised, except by implication, or incorporated the advertising styles of several decades in its ads, thus emphasising the ad, rather than the product. The term has subsequently been applied to any contemporary art or cultural activity which emphasises 'style' at the expense of content.

If the term had been restricted the above cases, then the term might have been a useful; but unfortunately the it has been extended, by people who want to use a buzz-word, not caring whether it actually means what they want to make it mean, to anything and everything in any way new, or perceived as new in art, culture and politics.

One of the most unfortunate of these extensions is to the area of literary and philosophical discourse known as post-structuralism — the leading light of which is the French philosopher Jacques Derrida. Another extension even more disastrously also includes the work of the French historian Michel Foucault. In fact it is a measure of the ignorance of the sort of people who are wont to make these extrapolations that these two writers are about as far apart as it is possible for two contemporaries to be, thought they are usually coupled together by angry (and ignorant) liberals, furious at their alleged joint attempt to destabilise Truth and Morality. As this work follows an anti-humanist trajectory it could risk being confused with some of the alleged misdemeanours of the two French thinkers. In fact the post-modern, or post-structuralist, assault on Truth and Morality is but the latest in a series of such attacks, beginning with the Greek Sceptic philosophers, and continuing through a long line of sceptic and antinomian thinkers. British liberals would be as well to remember that it was Hume, in the 1740s, who most famously demonstrated that morality is not able to be deduced from experience of the world, so such notions are by no means new. This work is indeed indebted to Foucault, though no more so than to Montaigne, for example, or Wittgenstein, or more especially Darwin, but hardly at all to the literary aestheticism of Derrida.

Consequently I should like to restrict my discussion of the postmodern to the areas first specified, where it turns out to be so clearly identified with the artistic style of Late Capitalism, it then becomes necessary to, as it were, answer it. I have argued above than the characteristics of Late Capitalism are latent within Middle and Early Capitalism, so clearly capitalism, and therefore modernity has not yet ended. It is easy to conceive of an awed aesthetic response to the latest enormities of modernity, a sort of eighteenth-century Sublime reborn. But just because, in post-Gatt times, there is alleged to be a free flow of information around the world which somehow transcends the mundane world of economic activity, and just because academics, or anyone else with a computer, can while away their time playing on Internet, should not mean that we are blinded to the continuance of all the destructive activity of capitalism of the past, or that which is still going on around us.

Nor is it as if the postmodern is a new phenomenon within modernity either, we can point, for example to the Aestheticism of late nineteenth century as another movement which stressed 'Play, ...Absence, Dispersal, ...Signifier, ...Desire, ...Irony, ...Immanence...' (Rose 49-51, quoting Hassan).

Finally the question of the post-modern is often coupled, as in the title of Rose's book, with the idea of the 'post-industrial'. If anyone is tempted by this concept they would be as well to remember than capitalism is still based solidly on industrial processes, and that no amount of clever advertising or fragmentation of signification will change this fact.

As this usage of the term 'post-modern' has ruined a perfectly good word, where, in this book, I want to refer to a time or a cultural space after modernity, I shall refer to it as 'praetermodern'.

2.5 I noted above the present widespread nostalgia for the post-war quasi-Keynesian settlement and a desire to return to it. Certainly as a means of curbing the excesses of the global market and its operators this seems very alluring. But it remains the case that the period of 1945-1970 was an unusual in the history of capitalism, one where the normal instability of the markets, which had been in evidence from the beginnings of capitalism to 1939 and has been much in evidence since 1970, was curbed in some measure. Nevertheless this was a calm, as it were, only on the home front, where, lulled with consumer durables, the newly wealthy middle-classes were rendered oblivious to the expansionist violence of capitalism in the Third World, and the concomitant ecological damage wreaked all over the globe. Nor are the beginnings of the Welfare State any example of a sort of 'softer heart' to be found in this period; the recommendations of the Beveridge Report in Britain, for example, were predicated upon continued strong economic growth.

The 'modernisation' associated with monetarist policies of the 80s and 90s has often been linked to right-wing politics. Certainly this was the case with the Republican administration of Presidents Reagan and Bush in the USA and with the Conservative governments of Margaret Thatcher and John Major in Britain. But elsewhere in the world it was social democratic parties which were the most eager to modernise, as, for example, with Bob Hawke's Labor government in Australia and David Lange's Labour government in New Zealand. In France even an avowedly socialist government was no less eager to modernise. These uncomfortable facts indicate that 'monetarism' and deregulation are not isolated eccentricities of the political right, but are within the mainstream of capitalistic thinking. (We might also in this context like to think of the abject rightwards shift of the British Labour Party while in opposition in the 80s and 90s). Thus 'modernisation' is not the prerogative of the political right and is simply one of the dynamics of capitalism, one which is always present in a modernistic temporality.

For it should be noted that although the modernisation of the economies of industrialised countries which occurred in the 80s and 90s was a cruel shock to the generations brought up under quasi-Keynesian policies, it represents no more than a return to some of the conditions which most people in the industrialised world had to endure under the first phase of capitalism and which most people in developing countries still have to endure.

Finally I should like to offer a simple sociological explanation for one element of the   prestige that economic growth, the Market &c &c still enjoy. After the Second World War birth-rates in many Western countries (particularly the United States) picked up as returning servicemen displaced women in the workforce and started families; the general prosperity and optimism of the post-war years also encouraged larger families. This is the 'baby-boom', which began in the late 1940s and lasted until birth-rates began to decline again in late 50s. It is this generation of people, who began to come to adulthood from the late 1960s onwards, who now constitute the managerial, political and bureaucratic echelons of modernity, and are set to hold on to this power for at least another twenty years. Their upbringing was in the bright and prosperous world of the 50s and 60s, and consequently, although their entry into the institutions of modernity was at a time of crisis, for them Capitalism and the Welfare State represent the ideals of a just and efficient society. Indeed the crises of late Capitalism have probably instilled in most of them a determination, either to see what is valuable, in their opinion, in modernity saved and reinstated in some future liberal paradise, or to see thedynamic potential of the Market released from its bureaucratic shackles and allowed to perform its miracles.

Since there are, compared to the subsequent generation, so many baby-boomers, their hold on the upper positions in most institutions and organisations is likely to more prolonged than if theirs had been a less numerous generation (the fact that birthrates have slackened in their growth from the 1960s onwards is an

MAGDALEN COLLEGE LIBRARY

excuse used to justify the scaling back of many of the institutions of the Welfare State). It is also the reason why the next generation has generally found it so difficult to obtain a foothold in any of these institutions, and why the sort of doubts and qualifications represented by protest and green politics have found such a poor reception in public counsels. It follows also that those of the subsequent generation whom the baby-boomers have allowed into their organisations are those who resemble them in all their delusions. Nor is only the machinery of government and commerce which is under the control of this caste, but even non-governmental organisations, such as those connected with nature conservation and the environment, the places one would least expect to find this caste, are staffed with them.

This baby-boomer generation is an extraordinarily dull, stolid, selfish, materialistic and dumbly liberal administrative cadre, blessed with a purblind ideology and bereft of any notions of public or societal duty. (In fact it could be argued that such notions have been replaced in late capitalism by the reality that consumerist behaviour *is* true public service, cf Milton Friedman's *obiter dictum* 'The only social duty is to maximise profit').

I have found, when I try to make the arguments of this book, or similar ones, the most extraordinary resistance, the most illiberal reception, even from those people whom one would expect to show them at least courtesy, such as academics. I have a feeling that it would have been much easier to make these arguments say in the 1930s, or the 1830s than now, and this is, once again, so contrary to what one might expect as to draw one up sharply and to prompt a rethink of what modernity's special qualities are. On the other hand I must confess a certain amount of glee at proposing in this work such a comprehensive slaughtering schedule for so many sacred cows — works like *Modernity, pace* the blurb writers for pornographic novels, are where all the taboos are *really* broken.

Chapter Three:
The Subjectivity of Modernity

Thus far in this work I have been making all the theoretical and rhetorical moves towards a comprehensive critique of modernity on account of its excesses: its commitment to a greater and greater consumption and its expansive, colonising imperative, which brings larger and larger areas, cultural and geographical, under its sway.

There is, however, a major problem in the way of such a critique and although I believe I can side-step this, and come up with a much more cogent critique of modernity than its usually offered, it will be necessary to spend the rest of this book dealing with the problem. And it is appropriate to introduce the problem at this point, when I begin to discuss the subjectivity of modernity.

3.1 If a temporality is the way in which time is socially structured (§1.3), then a subjectivity is a particular way of structuring and expressing individual and social experience. It is usually the case that a particular dominant subjectivity is associated with a particular dominant temporality, although like temporalities subjectivities are best though of as superimposed. However I shall be arguing that the subjectivity of modernity, backed up by the political, economic and cultural power of modernity is in a position to be more dominant than any other subjectivity in history.

In the last chapter I described how the industrial modernisation and restructuring of Taylor, Ford and those who imitated them, created the characteristic mass consumption society of the late twentieth century (§2.3). Although most people who would indignantly deny that their attitudes and habits are shaped by their circumstances a dispassionate sociological review of social habits, practices and attitudes (like those undertaken in France by Pierre Bourdieu) would reveal precisely that the temporality of modernised industry and it concomitant governmental and media structures and world-view produced by these *does* have an overwhelming influence on individual behaviour, and may indeed define it.

25

Modernity

The effects of a modernised temporality on individual behaviour, however, is more difficult to recognise and describe because of an obstinate habit of modern thought, which assumes that we can both be social actors and at the same time reflect from some neutral vantage point upon our actions (anthropology is always about everyone else, and the more 'primitive' the better). This belief arises from two considerations: the first is that as we are generally more materially developed than any previous society we naturally assume we are somehow better (§1.1); the second consideration is that we feel ourselves to be free agents, in the way which other peoples do not necessarily feel themselves to be. Yet this belief is not an independent consideration, but as subjects of modernity we necessarily feel our selves to be free, in the same way as the subjects of fatalistic cultures feel themselves entirely to be at the whim of Fate.

Thus it is the case that when we reflect upon ourselves the fact that we are workers and consumers within modernity is forgotten, and modernity as the social 'given' into which we are born, as other people are born into hunter/gatherer societies, traditional agricultural societies &c &c, is elided in our minds. In fact, although we generally have some freedom, and some freedom in excess of that which other societies allow their members, for example the freedom to live where we like, to follow what career we like, and so on, these are always more circumscribed than we care to admit. Moreover the one conclusive freedom we could have, which would prove that we were indeed truly free agents, that is, that freedom not to be our (modernistic) selves, is the one freedom we do not have, and the one freedom we cannot grant to anyone else. The practical expression of this freedom would be the freedom to live outside the capitalist world-economy. Examples of peoples who have tried (from indigenous people trying to hold on to their land and their lifeways, to hippy communes in developed countries) show how difficult and without recognition these attempts are.

This study, it will be objected, tries in fact to do what I have just claimed is impossible, namely to transcend the subjectivity of the culture to which its author belongs. My reply to this charge I would say that I do try to stand back and take a careful look at modernity *as it were* from the outside. However, unlike a host of philosophers from Kant onwards, I do not claim that anything I say can actually describe what it is like 'on the outside', my being there is more a rhetorical position than an exercise in critical philosophy. However, to anticipate chapter nine and my conclusion, I would say the only proper prescription that can logically be made in speaking from such a position is a recommendation that those mechanisms which permit modernity's global reach should be wound back, so that in future whatever the philosophers, or the statesmen or business-men say, or do, do not appear to be general statements of truth, and cannot be taken other than as culturally specific pronouncements, or recommedations for locally effective actions.

In any case those to who try to argue, from a liberal perspective, that there can be no such thing as an independent, over-arching, theoretical discipline, such as critical philosophy, are being disingenuous. For no one doubts that that there can be no such thing; what there can be, however, is a critical discipline which is *traditionally credited* with a theoretical, or regulatory function, *within modernity*. And indeed there is, perhaps philosophy, but more especially history and natural history (or ecological science). This study draws on insights from all three disciplines.

3.2 In fact the notion of personal freedom is not only wholly modernistic, but it is linked with the other discourses of modernity from their inception. At the same time as industrialism was beginning to transform the economy of Britain, the first Romantic poets were beginning to celebrate individual freedom and to criticise the materialism of contemporary society. And indeed this has been what might be termed the 'aesthetic' response to modernity ever since. Certainly the idea that there is a large and generous conception of human nature and its capabilities, purged of all the materialism of society, is a very alluring one. Surely, we might think, all the dogma of an orthodox liberal/Hegelian modernity can be set aside ultimately, and modernity saved from its crass mis-reading in economic terms of its fundamental dynamic?

I believe that this is one blind alley of criticism which must be refused, for the notion of individual freedom and the cognate one of economic development are inextricably intertwined within modernity, and have been so since its very beginnings. To demonstrate this we should look to Adam Smith's *Wealth of Nations* (1776), which is well-known as the foundation of modern economics, but contains also several interesting reflections on Smith's view of human nature (Smith was actually a Professor of Moral Philosophy, and the discipline of economics grew out of this discipline). At one point in the book, for example, Smith, begins to wonder exactly what it is that drives the machinery of commerce and capitalism:

> With regard to profusion, the principle which prompts to expence, is the passion for present enjoyment; which, although sometimes very violent and very difficult to be restrained, is in general only momentary and occasional. But the principle which prompts to save, is the desire of bettering our condition, a desire which, though generally calm and dispassionate, comes with us from he womb, and never leaves us till we go into the grave. In the whole interval which separates those two moments, there is scarce perhaps a single instant in which

MAGDALEN COLLEGE LIBRARY

> any man is so perfectly and completely satisfied with his situation, as to be without any wish of alternation or improvement of any kind. (II iii (363))

As if this was not enough, Smith had diagnosed the same phenomenon in different and more extreme terms earlier in the book:

> The desire of food is limited in every man by the narrow capacity of the human stomach; but the desire of the conveniences and ornaments of building, dress, equipage and household furniture, seems to have no limit or certain boundary. Those, therefore, who have the command of more food than they themselves can consume, are always willing to exchange the surplus ... for gratifications of this other kind. What is over and above satisfying the limited desire, is given for the amusement of those desires which cannot be satisfied and which seem altogether endless. (I ix ii (183))

In other words what drives capitalism is the desire for material well-being and goods—but such is the dynamism of this latter-day avarice that it cannot be described within any limits and properly has 'no limit or certain boundary'. A little earlier than this David Hume had described the requisites of a class of good capitalists thus: 'Their greed must be made insatiable, their ambition beyond measure, and all their vices profitable for the common good' (quoted in Beaud 68).

What was happening at this time was the replacement of a static idea of subjectivity (that a person occupied a particular place in society because of his or her birth, and the 'natural' character and disposition that went with this birth and upbringing) with a dynamic one (that every person has a potential which he or she strives to fulfil, always, of course, understood within the Market). Even now one could not recommend the older view without being accused of being elitist, absurd, unfair and discriminatory. Speaking personally I am so much a child of modernity that I find it very uncomfortable to think of personality in pre-modern terms, and yet I am no less unhappy with the modernistic version, which, it will be understood, condemns the majority of humanity to the status of failures (those who did not fulfil their potential), without even the consolatory role of forelock-tugger. For whenever the subjectivity of modernity is explicated it is always in crass and absurd statements such as this by US Vice-President Al Gore, in a speech to the World Poverty Conference in Copenhagen in March 1995 (a joke circulated shortly after this lavish event to the effect that the only poverty on display was poverty of thought). In the course of his speech, the Vice-President said:

> In our view, only the market system unlocks a higher fraction of the human potential than any other form of economic organisation and has the demonstrated potential to create broadly-distributed new wealth.

Symptomatic of this view is that there is only one human potential, though what for is not explained, presumably the Vice-President meant the potential to engage in the market system, which the market system certainly unlocks. Modernity and the market system would more accurately be described as the system which locks up practically every human potential, except one.

3.3 Yet it may seem an exaggerated view that modernity prevents the delineation of the vices, we can, after all, still meaningfully describe people as 'greedy', or 'slothful'. Why is it that this modernistic avarice compromises a critique of itself from an enlightened moral perspective?

To answer this we must consider a Christian moral perspective, itself strongly indebted to the classical Stoic tradition; this not to recommend necessarily such an analysis, but merely to think of the antecedents to Smith's analysis of human wants. The classic Christian moral perspective was to think of humans as prey to the Seven Deadly Sins — Anger, Lust, Avarice &c — which are headed by Pride, the epitome of them all. If each of these sins is a desire *for* a particular thing, as Lust is a desire for concupiscence, Avarice is a desire for wealth and so on, then Pride is just a general sort of overconfidence in one's self. The Enlightenment paradigm in which Smith was working had subsumed all these under the government of Reason, with the various failings now being considered an *immoderate* and *unreasonable* desire for something or other. However what is really so destructive of Smith's Enlightenment views of the economy is that there is 'no limit or certain boundary' to the desires he sees as central to capitalism. In other words not only are these desires unreasonable by definition, but they destroy the possibility of ever judging them by reasonable criteria.

Thus in place of desires *for*, modernity has unleased a sort of generalised Desire, which prowls hungrily about not only in poetic and philosophical texts (Hegel, Schopenhauer, Nietzsche, Freud &c), but amongst the board-rooms, cabinet rooms and exchanges of the world. And nowhere can there be any respite or island of calm preserved from Desire. Thus, strictly speaking modernity becomes a history of Pride, or, to use an analogous ancient Greek notion, of *hubris*: an economy of Desire which obliterates the proper limits of human activity, and invites retribution of some kind.

But more prosaically this transformation often fatally hinders a critique of modernity, since, so great are the crimes of modernity that the only solution often seems to be an exaggerated criticism which confuses the characteristics of modernity with the cussedness of things in general, and ends up swinging towards hair-shirts and gruel in an ecstasy of anti-materialism which is a parody of modernity's own extreme nature. We might say that Desire, in the generalised sense we noted above as a characteristic of modernity, is not the prerogative of economic and philosophical rhetoric and practice alone.

3.4 However, beyond this there is another, more important, reason why critiques of modernity are often flawed. Adam Smith noted in the first passage I quoted in §3.2 that compared to the 'violent' passion which prompts immediate expenditure, the desire to save is 'calm and dispassionate'. He might have added that this is because it is concerned with future gratification, that is, our decisions now are made with a view to future prosperity, which is why we can tolerate economic austerity, so long as it is coupled with the promise of 'jam tomorrow'. This is also why, incidentally, capitalism appears so reasonable when contrasted, as in the passages quoted from Adam Smith above, with an older temporality of acquisition and symbolic and public expenditure (this is Weber's 'rationalisation' (25)).

Often an 'anti-materialist' critique of modernity is framed in the very same way, that is, it lays down that modernity at present is mired in its materialism, but in the future the economic gains it has secured can be used as the basis on which to build a juster society, one purged of its materialism. In the same way we are always told that in order to afford more social justice, a better provision of health care, more comprehensive welfare arrangements &c &c we need a 'bigger cake', so every one can have larger slices. I hope that I am not spoiling anyone's hopes and expectations by pointing out that the consummation of a non-materialistic society will never occur, just as a 'larger cake' does not produce any more social justice, and often less (Robinson 245), than was enjoyed before.

One such misguided expression of the hope for the future is John Maynard Keynes' essay 'The Economic Possibilities of Our Grandchildren' (1930). Here Keynes distinguishes between two sorts of needs, 'absolute' and 'relative'. The absolute needs are those 'we feel ...whatever the situation of our fellow human beings may be' (365), whereas the relative needs are 'those ...we feel ...only if their satisfaction lifts us above, makes us superior to, our fellows' (365). Keynes imagines that at 2% growth, within a hundred years *'the economic problem may be solved'*, that is, *'the permanent problem of the human race'* (366, italics in original). This will then allow people to live more fully: to work less (367-68), not to have to love money (369) and not to have to defer their pleasures (370).

However, Keynes warns in a notorious passage, to accomplish this goal the 100 years of economic growth will be necessary first:

> But Beware! The time for all this is not yet. For at least another 100 years we must pretend to ourselves that fair is foul and foul is fair; for foul is useful and

fair is not. Avarice and usury and precaution must be our gods for a little while longer still. For only they can lead us out of the tunnel of economic necessity into daylight. (372)

In fact, as readers will doubtless have realised, the high levels of economic growth achieved after World War 2 mean that Britain has already reached the stage Keynes said would be necessary to reach before capitalism can stop developing, but growth has become an end in itself (in fact it always was), 'relative needs' have become 'absolute' ones (indeed there are no grounds for making this distinction in the first place (§4.4)), and only a fool, or a green thinker, would risk saying in public that economic growth must stop. At the same time this does not stop critics positing a similar future paradise to Keynes, but none that I have heard recently is so precise as to give a date to this future state, as Keynes did to his.

3.5 Beyond these criticisms there is an even greater problem with a discourse which seeks to criticise modernity for its inhumanity. Not only is the criticism flawed by the fact that it cannot help but draw upon a generalised Desire, but the figure in whose name the criticism is being made, namely The Individual, has no absolute basis and is a creation of modernity itself, as the vehicle for modernistic Desire. (Perhaps, incidentally, this is why Freud, when he analysed Desire, finally came to see it as a desire for death and annihilation). Thus it is easy to see how notions of material and human progress are so often linked and are not, strictly speaking, able to be disentangled.

As if this were not bad enough a further bar to critique is that many of the terms of critique, particularly its moral vocabulary ('the cruelty of modernity' &c) are also entirely the production of the society of the critic and have little transcultural relevance. There is no blue-print for an ideal social paradigm laying down that the duties of society are 1. Not to be cruel, 2. .... Few cultures have in fact made it a virtue to be cruel, except in war, but the point is that definitions of cruelty differ from culture to culture. In fact the most we can say when comparing societies is that they have a certain 'family resemblance' (as Wittgenstein put it), principally that they *are* paradigms of social relations, not idealist agenda (§5.1).

This position which I have just alluded to, the so-called 'anti-humanist' one (as though its proponents were any less interested in problems which affect human beings as their liberal and Marxist counterparts) has been furiously attacked for destroying the basis of any resistance to modernity's excesses (would the liberals and Marxists had saved their venom for those excesses). I don't think it does, and think it also helps to clear away a great deal of redundant argument. I also think that an ethical critique of aspects of modernity is not impossible, because a temporality and subjectivity cannot obliterate everything that has gone before. Enough

MAGDALEN COLLEGE LIBRARY

cultural resources survive for a strong critique of modernity from, for example the direction of the Common Law, from the ideas of Natural Justice (which derive from Roman Law and are very useful in, for example, framing transcultural human rights protocols), a version of the much contested notion of 'reason', or from a sort of secularised Christian notion of justice, to name only a few areas which might yield useful tools.

Indeed were modernity like any other social paradigm only a 'local' criticism would be needed, and the positive steps which have occurred to help soften the brutality of capitalism could be celebrated and extended. Such would be the task of cultural critics if all time were ours, and indeed any *general* critique of modernity would, in this case, be a liability, since there are no criteria for judging between different social paradigms, *except* the external effects of the temporality in question (§5.3). However, if we can say that social systems have as their sole 'ethical' end their own continuance, then we can also say that modernity, because of its instability and expansiveness and the destruction of the natural systems and resources necessary for its own continued existence, is profoundly unethical, and, uniquely amongst social systems *needs* a comprehensive critique. A further indictment of modernity would be that because of its instability, its expansionist imperative and its destructiveness it also compromises the continued existence of any other social system in the world (§7.2). This is the critical position which will be sketched out in the remainder of the book.

MAGDALEN COLLEGE LIBRARY

Chapter Four:
Marx and Marxism

4.1 At this point it would be useful to discuss Marx and Marxism for two reasons. The first is that any radical opposition to the workings of capitalism in the last 100 years has usually come from a socialist or Marxist perspective, so it will be interesting to examine what the grounds for such an opposition are. The second is that such an investigation can, ironically, illuminate further several aspects of our discussion of liberalism in the previous chapter.

I shall be arguing in this chapter that, contrary to popular opinion, Marx's understanding of modernity is fully in keeping with a modernistic subjectivity, and that the history of twentieth-century Marxist regimes has demonstrated this very nicely.

This is ironic in view of the fact that in *Das Kapital* (1st ed 1867) and other works Marx produced some of the most sharp and accurate descriptions of the dynamics of capitalism, in particular capitalism's habit of revolutionising prior temporalities (in Marx's terminology 'relations of production'), and its expansive, colonising impulse. Those familiar with Marx's ideas will already have recognised my indebtedness to them in chapter one and elsewhere.

4.2 On the other hand signs of Marx's modernity are everywhere and particularly in his earlier works. The first part of *The Communist Manifesto* (1848, written with Engels) is a long paean to the bourgeois' overturning of the feudal order and its dynamic role in revolutionising modes of production, which has as its thesis: 'The bourgeoisie has played a most revolutionary role in history'.

Now that this revolution had occurred the proletariat, according to Marx, had only to discover itself, flex its muscles and transform the selfish capitalist system into a communist one which would 'widen, ... enrich [and] ... promote the existence of the labourer'. Thus, far more explicitly than any liberal theorists, (it is only latent in Hegel's work), Marx and Engels set out a dialectic scheme, with the feudal and aristocratic period of the European Middle ages being the thesis, the

MAGDALEN COLLEGE LIBRARY

bourgeois revolution the antithesis, and the future communist society the synthesis: 'in bourgeois society, therefore, the past dominates the present; in communist society, the present dominates the past'. Uncomfortable as the recognition will be it needs pointing out that the future utopia of Marx and that of liberalism differs only in the question of private property and the question of whether the individual or the class is the basis of society. Furthermore, anyone who rejects Marx's concept of classes true to themselves will logically have to reject the idea of individuals true to themselves, as both the Class and the Individual emanate from the same discursive locus.

4.3 An interesting question which the above raises is the nature of the world which the proletariat are promised in the penultimate sentence of the *Manifesto*. It will be apparent that this world is one which has already been structured for them by modernity, as an earlier passage of the book makes clear:

> The discovery of America, the rounding of the Cape, opened up fresh ground for the rising bourgeoisie. The East Indian and Chinese markets, the colonisation of America, trade with the colonies, the increase in the means of exchange and in commodities generally, gave to commerce, to navigation, to industry, an impulse never before known, and thereby, to the revolutionary element in the tottering feudal society, a rapid development... Modern industry has established the world market, for which the discovery of America paved the way. This market has given an immense development to commerce, to navigation, to communication by land. This development has, in its turn, reacted on the extension of industry; and in proportion as industry, navigation railways extended, in the same proportion the bourgeoisie developed, increased its capital, and pushed into the background every class handed down from the Middle Ages.

In his later work (including *Kapital*) Marx grew more intolerant of the inhumanity and brutality of capitalism. Yet it is fair to say that his concerns remained always Eurocentric ones — for, like Hegel, he believed that Europe, was the geographical space where human self-awareness and the progress of the human spirit had achieved its most advanced form, although he, unlike Hegel, saw this in class, not individual, terms. Thus in *Kapital*, after discussing the problems which 'settler' colonies (ie USA, Australia) have in creating a class of wage labourers, Marx comments:

> However, we are not concerned here with the conditions of the colonies. The only thing that interests us is the secret discovered in the new world by the political economy of the old world ... that the capitalist mode of production and accumulation ... have for their fundamental condition the annihilation of self-earned private property; in other words in the expropriation of the labourer. (VII, xxxiii (383))

In other works Marx shows as little interest in pre-modern temporalities, as in the passage cited above these are no sooner mentioned than they are destroyed by capitalism so that eventually, in Marx's scheme, capitalism itself can be superseded. This is a particularly marked feature of those portions of the *Grundrisse* manuscript which have translated under the title of *Pre-Capitalist Economic Formations* (ed Hobsbawm). This interpretation of Marx's work is backed by the pieces selected by Avermi in his *Karl Marx on Colonialism and Modernisation*. Although in most of the pieces Marx is sharply critical of imperialism, as practised by the European powers of his day, yet he almost always writes disparagingly of pre-capitalistic economies. Most famously he wrote of the effects of British rule in India in 1853:

> Now, sickening as it must be to human feeling to witness these myriads of industrious patriarchal and inoffensive social organisations disorganised and dissolved into their units, thrown into a sea of woes, and their individual members losing at the same time their ancient form of civilisation and their hereditary means of subsistence, we must not forget that these idyllic village communities, inoffensive though they may appear, have always been the solid foundation of Oriental despotism, that they restrained the human mind within the smallest possible compass, making it the unresisting tool of superstition, enslaving it beneath traditional rules, depriving it of all grandeur and historical energies. (88)

And continued in the same vein for several more enormous sentences. In another report on India for the *New York Daily Tribune* he wrote: 'England has to fulfil a double mission in India: one destructive, the other regenerating — the annihilation of the old Asiatic society and the laying of the material foundations of Western society in Asia' (125). And elsewhere in his writings he lays down that the rest of the world must be brought under European domination in order that the inevitable progression of humanity towards a socialist future can be accomplished (eg 439, 448).

Thus is it correct of Avermi, in his Introduction, to underline that the 'Asiatic Mode of Production' is Marx's worst nightmare, insofar as 'stagnant Asiatic despotism' (432), is the direct enemy of the dynamics of (European) history (11, 33-34).

4.4 There is another problem with Marx's work, however, which is, if anything, even more chronic and it is one, again, in which a strong similarity with liberalism emerges. One of the most admired sections of *Kapital* (perhaps because it occurs very early on in the work) is one where Marx discusses the 'commodification' which modernity inflicts on things, people and social relations (I i (4)). Put very simply Marx believes that modernity reduces things, people and social relations

MAGDALEN COLLEGE LIBRARY

to the status of exchangeable items on the world-market. Thus the commodity loses its relation with the labour which produced it and becomes merely an empty sign of that labour. As it stands this is a brilliant description of what might be called one aspect of the cultural poetics of modernity and it explains how, for example, western consumers can be so detached from the outcome of their consumption. The western consumer cannot see the cheap cotton shirt, for example, in terms of the ecological damage intensive cotton production entails in, say, India. Nor can s/he see in it the social injustice of the cotton factories and the sweat-shops in the Third World, or, as is increasingly likely, in 'the home country' itself. Instead, for him/her, it is simply a shirt, an article of fashion and social display.

However the notion of commodification and Marx's allied notion of 'alienated' labour (that the modern wage labourer have that portion of their labour which supports the reproduction of capital 'stolen' from them) cannot function as a fundamental critique of capitalism for this reason: that there are nowhere any 'objective relations of production' which can be used to contrast the false relations which modernity sets up. In describing pre-capitalist communities as 'real' (*Pre-Capitalist Economic Formations* 104), or describing them up as characterised by 'objective relations of production' (97) Marx is tapping into the common nineteenth-century belief that 'primitive' societies somehow represent archetypal, and therefore more authentic, societies (Kuper 72-73). In fact all human societies are equally socially complex (simply more or less extended, or more or less technologically advanced) and in all of them labour and the 'relations of production' are socially structured, not in a natural relationship with anything. Or, in the terminology I have used elsewhere in the book, labour and 'relations of production' are structured according to the temporality and subjectivity, or collocation of temporalities and subjectivities which obtain at the particular time and place in question.

In fact to digress for a moment it could well be that the Hegelian belief that every culture has a 'spirit' which it struggles to develop, is a very bad generalised description of pre-modern cultures, which, by and large, were heterogeneous and contingent rag-bags of cultural components. On the other hand it could be that this model is a very good one for modernity, only instead of concentrating all its resources and social structures towards developing the human spirit, it concentrates them towards the development of capital instead. Marx grasped this, but then swam with the tide and saw in economic development a less crassly Romantic humanism.

Thus a critique of modernity for its lack of authenticity is simply a critique of modernity for being modernity, which is no critique. The only two things we can critique modernity for are the habit it has of subverting and abolishing other social systems and its likely prejudicing of its own future resources. And, as noted above (§3.5) these are the two criticisms I will be using in the remainder of this book. All this is not to say of course that one cannot say that workers are underpaid for their work (as, comparatively, most are), or that 'the management' is not largely overpaid (as it usually is), or that a less extended society, one where production and distribution are more nearly located would not be one better able to conserve natural resources and that such a society would not be better placed to deliver social justice, but these are different matters, a different critique, a 'local' one.

4.5 Thus far we have been treating Marx as a synecdoche for Marxian communism as it has manifested itself in the twentieth-century. This is unfair insofar as neither Marx nor Engels ever went into much detail as to what a future communist society might look like or do, and it was therefore left to subsequent luminaries such as Lenin, Trotsky and Mao to make their own extrapolations from Marx's work. At the same time, however, all Marxist thought has appealed to Marx for its authority, in much the same way as the various strains of Christianity have always appealed to the life and teachings of Jesus for their authority. And just as new developments in Christianity often appeal to the New Testament for their inspiration, so Marxist thought has always returned to Marx for inspiration and renewal, as, most recently with the work of Louis Althusser in the 1970s.

It is interesting, however, to see how twentieth-century Marxism has fallen foul of contradictions of Marx's own work. Despite the fact that the treatment of pre-capitalist societies is so fraught with contradictions in Marx's work Marxism has arisen most spontaneously in pre-capitalist and colonised countries. This is in defiance of the fact that Marxian analysis fitted or fits these countries like a three-fingered glove. As an example of how Marxist analysis cannot take account of colonial or post-colonial situations I cannot resist reporting how I once heard a leading Australian Marxist, challenged to define Aboriginal Australians in Marxist terms, reply that they were clearly *Lumpenproletariat*!

Nevertheless the appeal of Communism in these contexts is that it is the nearest thing in Western political philosophy to an opposition to capitalistic modernity and this is no doubt the reason why it is so often seized upon. Though I would argue that this move is simply the sign of a deeper level of colonisation for rarely have indigenous political theories, such as Gandhi's rural development, been put forward to contest modernity. It is notable that Gandhi's model was soon abandoned by Nehru and his post-independence government in favour of orthodox socialist industrialisation.

Thus, where it is practicable, the model followed in newly socialist or 'post-colonial' socialist societies has been that of rapid industrial development, to bring forward the socialist future by the European method. This has been most obvious in the 'undeveloped' provinces of the former Soviet Union from the 1930s onwards and in the People's Republic of China since 1949; in both cases modernisation was of a scale and an inhumanity which defy belief and were more rapid than anything that occurred in the West. It should also be pointed out that the results of this development were and are a graver ecological degradation than occurred in the West, if only because the resources available were much larger and were comparatively less degraded than similar locations in the West before development begin.

So, bearing in mind the economic development which communism always entails, except in the very least developed parts of the world, it would be just as accurate to say that instead of the official version of the Cold War between Communism and Capitalism of 1950-1990, there was simply a struggle for precedence between two rival versions of Capitalism. Why the western, liberal version prevailed (or, to be more accurate, *seems*, in the very short term we have available, to have prevailed), are not worth discussing, in the same way that what might have been is always the least fruitful topic of discussion. But what we should note is that, as always, the 'failure' of communism is almost certainly not due to any innate inferiority, but to contingent factors, such as the 'head-start' in development which the West (especially the USA) enjoyed over the USSR.

What does need pointing out is the number of disturbing similarities between communism and capitalism, underlined by the current transformation of China, with communist system intact, into the world's 'fastest growing economy'. The first is that, just as liberalism's vision of a juster society of the future is always infinitely deferred, so Marx and Engel's vision of a future socialist society where the state will have 'withered away' never seemed like eventuating either. Secondly, just as the West's economic development was underpinned by a ruthless colonialism, so Moscow's satellites functioned in much the same way, as a communist empire. And if this empire in the wider sense was ultimately a drain on Soviet resources (ie propping up Cuba), its inner empire (Eastern Europe, Siberia, Central Asia) can be compared to the Western colonial and post-colonial systems. The Chinese 'rape' of Tibet is another case in point. Finally we should note that, as inept as Marxist analysis by class is, and one explanation for the appeal of communism to 'underdeveloped' countries is that only there are mass-classes still not fragmented by *embourgeoisement*; yet the Western classification of individual wants and rights is often as inept and divisive when applied to pre-capitalist societies.

4.6 Earlier (§4.4) I noted that a socialist critique of modernity could only be a local one, concerned with certain aspects of modernity, not with modernity itself. This is because socialism and communism still continue their involvement with large-scale industrial economic growth. It is of course possible to name socialist thinkers who have recognised the ecological constraints upon modernity (one thinks of Rudolf Bahro and Raymond Williams, amongst others). I also believe that a movement to alter the course of modernity would be logically accompanied by a political philosophy which stressed equality and comparative redistribution of wealth, possibly by means of reduced working-hours and a 'social wage'. These, one could argue are the most logical outcomes of the pre-modern ideologies of the Common Law (the Anglo-Saxon tribal egalitarianism), Christian ideas of justice, and Reason.

Nevertheless we have no right to try to predict what praeter-modernity might look like (§3.6), and it might turn out to be something entirely different from what we might hope or expect (a reappearance of the idea of hereditary rank and privilege, for example).

Furthermore, it may also be that proponents of 'green' politics and a move beyond modernity have to down-play considerably the egalitarian and redistributional aspect of their politics in order to win over the great middle-classes (§8.2.1, 2).

Chapter Five:

Hegenomy

5.1 One question which has been raised by the foregoing chapters and needs to be addressed at this point is the question of hegemony: how modernity produces and maintains its predominance. There is little mystery how modernity maintains its hegemony in the traditional sense, that is its political control over much of the world; this is a product of brute economic strength, which is only occasionally shaken by obstinate rebels or guerilla-groups. But I am thinking of hegemony in the sense invented by the Italian communist thinker, Antonio Gramsci; how is it that modernity captures and continues to enthral the 'hearts and minds' of its subjects?

For if, as Marx and many other thinkers of all shades of political opinion have thought, capitalism is inherently contradictory, then there should be no difficulty in getting people, or classes, to recognise this, to oppose capitalism and to overcome it. Indeed we should note that no social paradigm in history has been so consistently and fundamentally attacked from within by its own intellectuals. Given this, and the fact that capitalism has, obviously, not ended, then we must conclude that most of the opposition they proclaim is in fact contained within modernity's dialectic schemes of thought, and cannot be taken at face-value as fundamental criticism, as I have already argued (§§3.4, 4.2).

5.2 However I have also been arguing that capitalism is not in the least contradictory; as we saw in the last chapter it does not replace 'real' communities with 'false' ones, or 'objective relations of production' with 'subjective' (?) ones. Durkheim and other sociologists and anthropologists have realised that what the fact of being human (ie a member of the species *Homo sapiens*) entails is being socialised, conforming to the social *mores* and processes which obtain in one's society. The fact that there are, and have been, many different societies in human history, all with different schemes and 'rules', shows that the social rules which obtain in any particular society are contingent, historical artefacts, heterogeneous, various and illogical, but having one feature in common, namely that they *are* social rules, not natural behaviour.

In other words the essence of human society is that it is a social, not a natural fact, and does not exist in any simple, 'natural' relation to its supply of food and materials; nor is the production and distribution of these foods and materials any less the product of socialised relations. The fact that human societies are never in a full 'ecological fit' with their environment is demonstrated by Robert Bettinger, who points out the flaw in the 'neo-functional ecological' school of anthropology's view of hunter/gatherer societies. These anthropologists see hunter/gatherer societies as perfectly adapted to their environments, but the problem then remains of how to account for their origins, were they once less well adapted (6-7)? This view of hunter/gatherer societies also fails to account for why some such societies changed to agricultural ones. In fact hunter/gatherers' relationship to the environment, like that of all plants and animals, is not perfect and contains 'room for manoeuvre', otherwise any tiny ecological change would mean extinction.

In the short term, the most prominent feature of any society is usually a lack of change, insofar as there is little leeway for large social change. But in the long term societies can 'drift' as a result of an aggregate of social decisions divergent from the norm, whether simply social or in response to economic or ecological factors. However, like Darwinian evolution, cultural evolution can often be sudden and dramatic, though such changes are rare (§5.3). We can recognise both dynamics in modernity, the sudden switch to a capitalist temporality, followed by a long continuance of modernistic life-ways which can slowly produce social change (in the matter of Fordism, mass-consumption &c) but remains fundamentally within modernistic trammels in the absence of any imperative to change from outside, in the way of a rival political system, or massive ecological change.

5.3 It is worth examining some of the above considerations of how social change can occur in more detail. It is obvious that social customs and relations will change over time and the way they change is often connected with social 'drift', the best example of which is the way in which language changes over time, slowly once the printed word has established a standard, but in pre-printing times, more rapidly.

However it is also obvious that the general tendency is still for social conservatism; in one lifetime the shift in linguistic usage might not have been very large. Societies function most smoothly, and with as little stress for their members, when the behaviour of society's members is reasonably predictable—and this, rather than anything else, is the 'truth' of social relations.

MAGDALEN COLLEGE LIBRARY

In fact, to digress for a moment, this conservatism is more hopeful than it might appear, since it allows for the survival of pre-modern temporalities (perhaps as 'back-up systems') in even the most modernised society. For example many urban Aboriginal Australians, despite having lost land, language and rituals, still do not behave in anything like the same way as their European Australian peers.

But to continue the argument; granted all this, then it is obvious that total social changes will be very uncommon in human history — indeed I have argued that there have really only been two, the change from hunter/gatherer societies to agriculture and the change to a capitalistic temporality, though even these have allowed submerged former temporalities to survive to a certain extent (§§1.3, 1.4). The reason for this lack of change is that if a change is in the offing, particularly one which requires a complete change of lifestyle, then few people are willing to make the transition on their own, but wait for others to 'jump' first. When these transitions do occur then the reasons for them must be extremely compelling — indeed in the preceding paragraphs I have been assuming that all humans are entirely free agents, whereas, of course, very few ever have been, however they may have thought otherwise.

Apart from these two paradigm-shifts, the only total shifts in human history are ones caused by ecological catastrophes, fortunately rare, although some areas, eg China, or the Tigris/Euphrates valley, seem particularly prone to them.

Thus, to sum up the above two sections. One of the principle reasons for modernity's retention of its hegemony is the simple one of social solidarity — once the temporality of modernity is established it becomes impossible, perhaps unthinkable, to differ, to be so different as to want to stand outside the system. And in practical terms this means that most people are far too busy earning a living to want, or to be able to, change things, there being as yet no definite proof that any change in their way of life will bring any tangible rewards.

Finally we should add here a caveat: there is no sense at all in being essentialist about a particular culture, by insisting, perhaps on the particular features of one culture, or its characteristics. For there have been few cultures, probably none, which are entirely immune from external influence and most have been profoundly influenced by other cultures at some time or another. Like language, cultures change over time, though they do have a tendency to give the appearance of not changing, and this is probably how they appear to outsiders and insiders. Nor is modernity immune from influence by the cultures it has come in contact with; nevertheless there are different degrees of influence, some influences produce only superficial change, others more material changes. It would be my argument that the underlying features of modernity have remained unchanged throughout its history, and have not been modified by any other influence, whilst the influence that these fundamentals have exerted in turn is revolutionary in whatever manner and wherever this influence manifests itself in other cultures.

At this point we should observe that as capitalistic modernity is simply one social system amongst many which have existed, then it cannot be uniquely immoral or wicked, since social systems have no moral purpose, but are simply social systems. *However, by the same argument, modernity cannot be uniquely better either, but simply a social system, like the rest.* Historians of the future will, no doubt, be able to point gleefully to modernity's inevitable progression to ecological catastrophe. Indeed history is always in danger of reading like an inevitable progression, because change can be reported more easily than a lack of change, so the immediate, contributory causes, not the underlying ones, are usually reported as sufficient causes of historical events. However, no one *wants* ecological catastrophe, least of all the leaders of business, government &c. But locked into a social system whose long-term sustainability is extremely doubtful, it is not therefore any easier to change that social system, especially one which has the habit of losing sight of the ecological consequences of its consumption.

5.4 But to add a further sophistication to this argument we must invoke the idea of cultural capital, a form of capital which is not concerned primarily with money, but with social status. What cultural capital is and who possesses it are much disputed questions—certainly cultural capital is not identical with capital *per se*, witness how in Britain the *nouveaux riches* are derided for their vulgarity and the penniless old-aristocracy fawned over. However, although the 'ineffectual intellectual' certainly has more cultural capital than, say, the much richer estate agent, cultural and actual capital are rarely completely divorced. And this is because in modernity, as in other societies, the control of resources and technology is a part of the trappings of authority, and every reader will be able to think of examples in his or her own experience of how authority and prestige are connected with perks, foreign travel, high salaries &c, to bear this analysis out.

Moreover, since modernity is pre-eminently the paradigm which multiplies capital and technology, so it is hardly surprising that modernity is able to recruit leaders from other societies—both at its inception and at later stages, as, for example, in the twentieth century, when the leaders and the elites of 'under-developed' countries are rewarded for their cooperation with all the marks of traditional authority, namely wealth and technology. Penelope Schoeffel argues, for example, that in the Pacific Islands the chief men of society have translated their traditional obligation of providing for their dependents into a more modern one of operating in the modernistic business and trade sphere and extracting goods and profits from there (in Howe, 373). In these cases we may smile in superiority only to the extent that whereas the deal struck by these leaders usually does not benefit most of the people of their countries, the deal which the bourgeoisie have 'struck' only really concerns the top, say, 40% of the population of developed countries.

Until the 1960s any opposition to modernity within developed or undeveloped countries came from groups with no cultural capital: women, vagabonds, gypsies, small-holders, peasants, natives and savages. With the emergence of the Peace Movement in the 1960s an 'alternative' lifestyle has begun to have some sort of *kudos* — indeed it is said that applications for jobs with organisations such as Greenpeace now commonly outnumber those for 'city' jobs, at least in Britain. And this sudden acquisition of cultural capital can, I think, be attributed partly to the eternal fascination of Bohemia, but also perhaps to the adumbrations of ecological crises to come, which are now more apparent than ever. The situation is perhaps cognate with the emergence of the various Christianities during the later Roman Empire.

Another point which needs to be made in this connection is that modernity itself can have cultural capital, that is, people can work with it, or, not actively oppose it because they believe that it represents a genuinely better way of life than any other social system. And the poverty and degradation which characterises the societies of 'undeveloped' countries (in truth, entirely of modernity's own making) is then adduced as proof of this. One thinks of the US 'Peace Corps' of the 1960s, with its hundreds of fresh-faced volunteer-workers. In §2.2 I pointed out that since the Second World War capitalism has been inextricably linked in popular discourses and economic theory with democracy, which is perceived to be the master way of life for all human beings; I will have more to say about this in chapter eight.

5.5 Another reason why modernity is so apparently unshakeable is owing to the characteristic we mentioned before, of 'rationalisation' (§3.4). This means that whereas in earlier paradigms economic activity of the modern kind was optional, and not part of the rationale of society as a whole, within modernity everything within society is turned towards the business of developing capital. This is why, as Weber put it, capitalism, whilst being more rapacious, actually looks more rational than other societies.

Not only is this rationalisation concerned with the structure of capitalism itself (businesses, industry &c) but government plays a part too. Thus the wholesale regulation and supervision of society which now accompanies the citizen from cradle to grave, and which simply did not exist 200 years ago, has the effect of heightening the productivity of this citizen/economic unit. And thus it comes about that everything is expressed in terms of its economic benefit, as, for example, health costs are treated as part of 'keeping the work-force healthy' and so on.

Some recent writers have begun to celebrate this aspect of modernity and claim that 'Governmentality' is a good thing, because it guarantees a healthy, educated, well-regulated, and prosperous citizenry. The historical argument they use to justify themselves is that the Thirty Years War (1618-48), in which up to a third of the population in some parts of Germany were killed, taught German princes that religious strife was the only result of religiously-based societies. Henceforth states were secular and existed only for themselves, that is, for the good of their rulers and their citizens. This regime of governmentality antedated capitalism and cannot be identified with it. It has moreover a different trajectory, and has the power to modify capitalism substantially.

I believe that it is one of the most important tasks for an anti-modernistic political movement to re-open this split between government and modernity, since any future move towards a praeter-modern society will not entail anarchistic freedom and the liberation of the human spirit, but initially a very carefully thought out programme of government regulation and legislation. But first government must be severed from capitalism and its GDP fixation. In fact if there really is a separate trajectory for government it must lead this way, since modernity is fundamentally inimical to the continued existence of stable, prosperous societies.

However, to answer the simplistic argument for 'governmentality', which seem to me, as currently argued, to be simply a sophisticated form of liberalism. Government may well have a historical origin which precedes capitalism, but once capitalism begins its economic power will twist government to its own ends. This is obvious. Secondly, although government action has ameliorated some aspects of capitalism it cannot control the global reach of capitalistic barbarity; for example, child-labour in western factories has now been legislated against, but this has not stopped capitalism exporting child-labour. Thirdly government, under the Keynesian, and subsequent, dispensation is itself a powerful stimulator of economic activity (§2.2), and caught up in all the great drama of capitalistic modernity. Fourthly, if we say that in the seventeenth century Europeans stopped killing each other for the sake of religion and turned to the secular state and capitalism, then it seems a pity that the rest of the world had to suffer simply in order that Europe could solve an endemic problem; it would certainly have been better for the generality of the human race if religious wars had continued to the present day in Europe, preferably as bloody as possible (in fact what has happened is that wars *have* continued in Europe, *and we have had modernity*). Fifthly, governmentality is clearly just as eurocentric as classical liberalism, insofar as it celebrates the order and prosperity of modern societies, yet this can only mean the

MAGDALEN COLLEGE LIBRARY

core territories of modernity; if quizzed about developing nations and their (absent) order and prosperity, the governmentalists would presumably have to reply, 'Ah well, when the natives become civilised....'. Finally our prosperity and order are, as I have argued throughout this book, chimerical. Not counting the wars and social strife brought about by modernity in all parts of the world Amnesty International estimate that 1 million people a year are killed by their own governments (International Report 1995).

5.6 To sum up then: capitalistic modernity maintains hegemony by its brute economic force, but this is not enough to account for its almost universal acceptance. Other factors which contribute to this are social habits of conformity, together with the need to earn a living and have a quiet life, the linkage of cultural capital to capital and to capitalistic activity, the natural status which is argued for modernity and the world-economy, and governmental regulation and surveillance. These, more than any crude repression, are the oil which lubricates the wheels of commerce. Nor are they fundamentally different from the causes of social solidarity in other societies, though the scale of modernity is very different.

A final point is the question of how we think of modernity. In my view it doesn't really matter how we describe it, so long as we remember that what we are doing is applying metaphors to aid our understanding, rather than trying to give a firm description of the essential nature of modernity.

A reasonable model would see modernity as simply a very unfortunate paradigm shift. Why the bundle of cultural pre-dispositions, technologies and in-stitutions we call modernity *is* so destructive, or why it began in the first place, or whether pre-modern western culture was a uniquely nasty culture just itching to turn into modernity, as many green thinkers seem to think, are questions which would need much more discussion than the scheme of this book would allow. Suffice it to say that I believe that modernity was an accident—that it began was due to the 'givens' of western culture in the later eighteenth century and that it continued was due the unfortunate coincidence of the opening up of the American Mid-West, thus ensuring a dependable source of cheap food, but that it was not inevitable. I seems to me also that there is nothing wrong with our spiritu-ality or our attitudes, which are no worse, though no better, than anyone else's, they are simply tied to the wrong discursive and institutional loci. Thus it follows that we really don't need new attitudes, or new spiritualities, but that if we can shift our institutions and our ways of going about economic activity into a praeter-modern phase, our dispositions and our attitudes would then, governed by our circumstances, change, although, and this is another caution, in some unpredict-able way. In other words we need to spend less time agonising about our consciousnesses and more time in making sure that we don't continue on in our mad ways.

Another conclusion that can be drawn from this premise is that the institutions, instruments and technologies of modernity are on the one hand, ideologically neutral, in that they could be used in anti-modernistic paradigm (though there are a few things, like nuclear technology that seem to be very fittingly part of modernity and would be homeless outside it). On the other hand within modernity *everything* is co-opted into modernistic procedures. This is obvious when, for example, a well-meaning Australian government trains Aboriginal people in modern management techniques to take back to their remote communities! Even the most disinterested and apparent innocent practices, such as modern medicine, can be a part of modernity's hegenomistic imperative. This is seen most clearly when medicine and education are used to bring third-world people 'into the modern world', that is, into modernity. One is reminded of Tacitus's remarks in *Agricola* about the ancient Britons reaction to 'arcades, baths and sumptuous banquets': 'The unsuspecting Britons spoke of such novelties as 'civilisation', when in fact they were only a feature of their enslavement'.

Chapter Six:

Matters Ecological

6.1 In this chapter I should like to investigate the ecological constraints upon the continued economic expansion of modernity – the 'Ecological Crisis'. However, almost as soon as invoking the term 'Ecological Crisis' I should like to disown it. For although the 'Ecological Crisis' is a 'crisis' in the traditional meaning of the word, 'a decisive or vitally important stage in the course of anything', yet in the rhetoric of the international media a crisis is something quite different. In this context a crisis is some such set of circumstances *which is just on the point of resolution*, usually by some dramatic action or other. It needs hardly saying that such a view presupposes a very simplistic world-view, where such crises can be quickly resolved. However if, as I having been suggesting in this book, the present state of the world is due to the superimposition of a capitalistic temporality upon other, prior temporalities, then we would expect that the crises which crop up will be neither simple, nor susceptible to immediate resolution.

The danger of describing the ecological constraints on modernity as a crisis is that this will raise the expectation of dramatic and immediate solutions. Instead I shall be arguing that this crisis admits of no immediate solutions because the problems at the bottom of it are absolutely fundamental to modernity. As an example of the dangers of talking of crises we might note that during the late 80s two aspects of the Ecological Crisis, the destruction of the ozone layer and global warming, were big news, and international agreements on both issues were pending. After the signing of the Montreal Protocol on Chloroflurocarbons (CFCs) in 1987 (and the Amendments to it signed in London in 1990) and the Rio Agreement on greenhouse gases in 1992, the issues dropped from media attention, as though they had been solved. In fact these agreements did not include enough signatory countries, or go far enough in limiting the emission of greenhouse gases, respectively, to be of any great use at all. Moreover the (inadequate) targets set by the agreements have little chance of being met, as

Australia, for one, has recently admitted (August 1994), in respect of greenhouse gas emissions.

However the cessation of coverage of these problems has, I'm sure, convinced many people that these problems have now been solved and are no longer a worry. Worse, in the course of my research I have detected a notable falling-off in popular and scientific publications on these two problems, compared with the number of publications of the late 80s; evidently publishers and distributors of research funds no longer consider these problems of any great weight any more either.

There is also another problem with treating ecological constraints as 'a crisis', one related to the foregoing considerations. That is that if such constraints are set up as a crisis, then the expectation will be, failing any dramatic resolution, that an immediate ecological nemesis is at hand. In fact there is no consensus at all on when, or if, we will pass the point in the process of the degradation of resources and life-systems beyond which it will be difficult to maintain any technologically sophisticated society — it may already have happened, it may be decades off, the experiment of planet-wide ecological degradation has never been run before. If nothing dramatic happens in the short-term, the natural, but illogical, reaction on the part of many will be to assume that nothing dramatic ever will happen. The answer is something of this nature will definitely happen as a result of modernity's economic activity, but whether it begins to happen at the end of the week, or at the end of next century is impossible to tell. In fact research on past climatic and environmental changes indicates that the natural environment has a great deal of resilience in the face of changing conditions, but once a certain point is reached, then conditions change extremely rapidly.

6.2 Logically, however, no one can doubt that modernity's ethic of continued and unlimited economic growth will in the end come up against ecological limits. As the World Resources Institute's latest report puts it: 'The North's patterns of resources consumption are not environmentally sustainable... either for the region itself or as a model for the world' (4). However, there are a number of reasons why this admission is not seen as an imperative for action. Firstly the reality of these constraints can always be denied. As S.Kaneff has written:

> It is unfortunate that vested financial and intellectual interests are still able to question the relevance, significance and extent of the ecological effects now evolving as a result of deleterious human-environment interactions. Their attitudes continue the pattern usually followed by colonisers, developers, entrepreneurs, corporate policy makers and planners (and many others) whereby short-term gain overrides perceived long-term degradation—often on the

MAGDALEN COLLEGE LIBRARY

> grounds that the likelihood of such degradation has not been conclusively proved. Yet even though they insist on incontrovertible evidence that deleterious environmental consequences follow from proposed activities, most if not all of [the] decisions made and actions taken by these same groups and organisations ... are taken on 'inadequate' evidence, as few situations in the real world are favoured with the availability of 'complete' information. (49)

And to his observation we need only add that the view that science can 'conclusively prove' anything is a vulgar misunderstanding of science, and one which would not be supported by many scientists: science can provide only 'best fit' explanations, which are always in need of refinement (Ziman 35), most scientific research is concerned with estimating probabilities, not establishing certainties.

But there are a couple of attitudes here which need to be further disentangled. The first is that very few people are genuinely 'anti-environment' in that they would like to see natural habitats and natural systems in general destroyed for the sake of being destroyed. Indeed many people who are involved in ecologically destructive decisions are often concerned to visit 'unspoilt' parts of the world, or live in pleasant surroundings and to criticise other people's environmental destructiveness. What seems to be a better explanation is that the consequences of economic degradation are not fully present to those making the decisions, particularly as the worst environmental degradation is often 'exported' to third-world countries. Furthermore, as no consumption taxes, petrol rationing, electricity shortages have yet occurred in the most developed countries, then those in charge of making decisions are understandably under the impression that things will carry on as they do at present indefinitely. We should remember that we in the developed world are to an extent cushioned from economic realities: 'Consumption in the North includes a wide variety of goods and services associated with consumer culture, while in the South it focuses primarily on basic needs' (World Resources Institute Report 3). A further mentality which can be adduced here is the familiar 'I can develop this piece of land because there is plenty of rain-forest/woodland/similar habitat left in the region', a valid point in some cases, but only when not everybody is thinking it, as is the rule nowadays.

There is also the thought, which may be present to some decision-makers, that there is nothing any one decision-maker can do which will make any difference. That is, any individual or organisation or nation which does make environmentally prudent decisions is thereupon penalised by the rest of society, the business world or the international community. This is Michael Jacobs 'invisible elbow' of the market which pushes individuals and organisations, often against their will, into the most ecologically damaging solution to their problems (127). Modernity, as we have pointed out several times, is a complete economic and social system and very resistant to change in any of its dynamics. Thus any attempt to rein in the excesses of modernity is usually watered down, or postponed, as for example proposals for controlling CO_2 emissions at the April 1995 Berlin Climate Conference were fudged, to the understandable rage of several South Pacific and Indian Ocean nations who face imminent extinction in the face of rising sea-levels.

6.3 But a second reason why the need for environmental concern is often neglected is that the modernistic mindset is very much against having to admit to any short-comings in the face of the natural world. The dominant attitude within modernity seems to be that the natural world is there for us and for our exploitation and that nothing should stop us, even if the particular parts of the world developers and entrepreneurs are interested in belong to someone else. Thus there is, in the minds of many people, still the delusion that whatever ecological constraints exist can be surmounted by further technological advances, or religious transcendence.

This delusion is fuelled by the failure of the economic crisis predicted by an earlier generation of environmentalists to come to pass. These first-generation environmentalists expressed concerns that the world's resources, particularly coal and oil, were rapidly running out and would not sustain economic growth in the long-term (these concerns were expressed most notably in the Club of Rome's 1972 *The Limits to Growth* report on the question). In fact since then further exploration has revealed that ample resources of coal and oil remain and will last for many centuries to come. A few resources may soon run out, such as certain metals, and, ironically in view of the advocacy of nuclear energy as a sustainable energy source, uranium, but these are likely to cause few problems, as technology can find new materials to replace them.

However current environmental concerns are not of this nature, they are concerned not with the exhaustion of certain resources, the loss of which will prevent certain economic activities, rather these concerns are that various flows and systems of the biosphere may be on the point of being so modified or disrupted that any sort of human activity is made more difficult. Or, to put it another way, not with the future loss of the exchange value of certain commodi-ties but with the loss of traditionally unpaid-for use values inherent in the natural and social environments. And here technological advances are no help as these have the unfortunate property of require *more* energy and *more* resources, when the use of more energy and more resources is problem in the first place; this is what Deborah White calls: 'the... "technical fix", in which supposed "solutions" can generate unwanted ripple effects, provoking increasingly elaborate and destructive "remedies"' (52, also Headrich in Turner, 55, 65).

MAGDALEN COLLEGE LIBRARY

Although much has been written and published over the past thirty years on the various areas of environmental concerns it might be useful in this context to provide a brief outline of the major concerns, which I will do the in next seven sections. My statements about the various crises are meant as a simple summary and are not meant to be final, exhaustive or authoritative; for such information I refer the reader to, for example, Turner's volume, or the World Resources Institute's latest Report, or any one of a number of reports prepared by non-government and government organisations.

6.4 **Global Warming** is occurring because the increased levels of Carbon Dioxide (CO_2) and other gases such as Methane (CH_4) and CFCs which human activity has caused. These gases trap the sun's energy in the atmosphere more efficiently and a gradual rise in temperature ensues, rather like a greenhouse. The temperature of the Earth has varied in the past and CO_2 and the various greenhouse gases have played their part, but the current rise in temperature is entirely anthropogenic, as a result of the liberation to the atmosphere of the carbon previously locked up in timber, coal and oil, by the use of these substances as fuels. The concentration of CO_2 in the atmosphere increased by 25% in the period 1700-1985 and 50% of this increase has occurred in the last 30-40 years (Houghton and Skole in Turner, 401-405).

Since the late nineteenth century average global temperatures have increased by 0.45°, and the Intergovernmental Panel on Climate Change in its 1990 and 1992 reports predicted that if CO_2 concentrations double (which is expected to happen by 2025, if business as usual continues) then a rise of between 1.5° and 4.5° can be expected.

The real problem of global warming is not that everywhere is going to get 1.5°-4.5° warmer uniformly. Instead the weather patterns of the whole planet will change, some areas will become warmer or wetter, other will become colder or drier, in addition some places will become much windier. Generally the effect will be that of disruption as people have to learn very quickly to plant different crops, to use different cultivation techniques &c &c, and some areas will become un-inhabitable. The world is crucially dependent on the great wheat-growing areas of the world, notably the American Mid-West and the Russian Steppes; if these areas suddenly become unsuitable for wheat-growing then the world will face food-shortages on a scale never seen before. Moreover it is expected that the sea-level will rise, as Arctic and Antarctic ice melts; most of the world's most productive agricultural land and almost all its cities are at, or just above sea-level and the cost of defending, or abandoning, these will be enormous. Overall there will probably be less cropland and we can expect massive migrations and large-scale warfare as nations strive to adjust to new conditions.

In addition it is expected that as the tropical zones of the world expand, so tropical diseases such as malaria will expand into the temperate zones, especially as rising sea-levels will create more wetlands for mosquitos, the carriers of many of the worst tropical diseases, to breed in. Similarly tropical agricultural pests and crop disease are expected to increase.

Furthermore, all known feedback loops in global warming are positive (Houghton and Skole in Turner, 406, Cline 22-25). For example a vast quantity of peat is locked up in the perma-frosted tundra regions of the Northern Hemisphere. If this begins to warm up and thaw out they will release even more CO_2 into the atmosphere, and that very quickly. A similar, but even greater problem, is the amount of gas hydrates frozen underground in polar regions; these, if thawed, will quickly release enormous quantities of CH_4 (an even more powerful greenhouse gas than CO_2) into the atmosphere. Thus William Cline and other writers see the dangers in global warming not so much in the short-term, as in the long-term (200-300) years, when, as a consequence of feedback and continued CO_2 and CH_4 emissions the global temperature might have risen by 10°C.

And, needless to say, it is very difficult to do anything about global warming as power-generation by fossil-fuels is absolutely basic to modernity. Nuclear power has shown itself to be expensive, dangerous, unpopular and unreliable and the various alternative sources of energy mooted have not yet been perfected on the correct scale (and perhaps they are only suitable for small-scale and local power-generation). It is true that demand for power has levelled off in developed countries (Headrich in Turner, 56), but this will be more than made up for by the increasing use of power in developing countries. Moreover even if carbon emissions could be kept at their present levels then global warming will still occur; it has been estimated that it would take an immediate cut of 60-80% in emissions to stop warming completely (Cline 17). The Rio Agreement on greenhouse gas emissions, although important symbolically, is largely useless insofar as its targets are too modest, and in any case unattainable by many countries. Global warming will occur and its effects will no doubt affect, one way or another, the course of modernity.

6.5 **Ozone Depletion** occurs when the layer of ozone (O_3) in the upper atmosphere is attacked by CFCs and other anthropogenic gases. This ozone layer has the effect of shielding the earth from ultra-violet radiation. When the layer is depleted more ultra-violet light, and ultra-violet of several different wavelengths penetrates the atmosphere. Ultra-violet light is extremely damaging to skin-tissue and the eye, and an increase in it will result in thousands of extra cases per year of skin cancers and various kinds of eye-damage.

This depletion was first proved in the early 1980s when the famous 'hole in the ozone layer' over Antarctica was discovered. CFCs and the other ozone-destroying gases work best at very low temperatures, and in the antarctic winter they deplete much of the ozone over the south polar regions, in summer ozone from lower latitudes drifts back, repairing the damage. Recently a similar loss of ozone has been noticed over the Arctic, and the increase in ultra-violet from this source has the potential to affect the populations of the developed countries of the Northern Hemisphere.

What is extremely worrying about ozone-depletion is that it is so recent (CFCs and the other ozone-destroying gases have only been produced in quantity in the last thirty or forty years) and so extensive. It is also irreversible in the short-term. Its effects, besides those of forcing the populations of the higher latitudes to take extreme anti-ultra-violet precautions, will be to affect the vegetation of all parts of the world, as ultra-violet in slightly-increased doses stimulates plant-growth, in larger doses destroys plant-tissue, though not in all plants equally. How these changes will interact with those of global warming is anyone's guess. With ozone depletion, as with global warming , we see that the effects of modernity's industrial and economic activities is to create uncertainty and disruption.

Strangely enough the international treaty signed in Montreal in 1987 and amended in London in 1990 does do something worthwhile towards solving the problem; perhaps an indication of the perceived severity of the problem. CFCs, by the terms of this agreement, will be phased out in the short-term. Unfortunately many countries have not signed, and several developing countries, notably China and India, have indicated that, as the major use of CFCs is in refrigeration, and all the ozone-friendly alternatives are much more expensive, they will not be able to become signatories as they place improving the health and quality of life of their citizens before possible environmental deterioration.

6.6 The **general degradation of resources** is not to be confused with the worries mentioned above (§6.3) about the running down of stocks of fossil fuels. This was perceived simply as a danger to the continued growth of developed and developing economies, as the Club of Rome Report's title, *The Limits to Growth*, indicated. Had fossil fuels been depleted as feared then all that would have happened is that transport and manufacturing would have become much more expensive, and extensive use of power for manufacturing, domestic use and transport might have had to have been curtailed. However the degradation of resources I am discussing here concerns global systems, the failure of which would result in mass starvation. We, ie humanity, could cope with less manufacturing, transport &c &c, but it is difficult to see how we can cope with the loss of arable land, forests, fish-stocks and fresh water, to name only a few areas of concern.

Before detailing a few of these concerns there is another consideration to bear in mind. The degradation of resources is often not obviously a result of western capitalistic activity; it is usually carried out by the people on the spot (§1.4). And this has the unfortunate effect of making it easy to shift the blame for environmental degradation from modernity's minions to the local inhabitants. During the 1980s I often heard the view expressed that the sufferings of the Ethiopian people were 'their own fault', as it was they who had created the conditions which lead to mass-starvation with the onset of drought. Nor was Ethiopia ever colonised (except by the Italians briefly in the 30s and 40s) so there is no obvious causal relationship with capitalistic modernity.

The answer to this is firstly to point out that until the modern period (ie after 1800) there was little environmental degradation of any sort anywhere in the world. And those areas where there was such degradation, such as Europe and China, were usually areas under the control of some centralised state or economic system. (Indeed early modern Europe, with its chronic and periodic famines and epidemics must have been one of the most miserable places in the world at the time, despite 'the Renaissance' and 'the rebirth of the human spirit'). The second thing to point out is that if, as we have argued (§1.3), modernity represents a superimposition of a new temporality on prior, pre-modern temporalities, then it follows that modernity can often work by indirect means upon traditional societies. John Richards, for example, has pointed out how as early as the nineteenth century in China, Bengal, Burma and Ghana, all areas then outside Europe's direct political control, the expansion of modernistic colonialism created local 'settler' cultures which pushed agriculture into areas never before cleared (in Turner 166). And it is easy to see how this process is even more insidious in the present century, when as a result of the modernisation of agriculture, local people are deprived, by governments or large land-owners, of control over their own land. These dispossessed people then move to less suitable, more marginal areas and begin a desperate and unsustainable agriculture. The new plantations, geared to the cash economy and export market, are often no less disastrous ecologically, and the whole environment becomes more and more degraded. This process is obvious in such countries as Brazil, where it is penniless and dispossessed peasants who are used as the shock-troops in rainforest destruction, and the same process has operated in every part of the world, including Ethiopia.

Indeed Richards' idea of 'frontiers' is a very valuable model for thinking about the whole question of general degradation of resources. After pointing out that the area of arable land has increased world-wide by 466% in the last 300 years (Turner 162), he goes on:

MAGDALEN COLLEGE LIBRARY

> The unremitting twin drives for domination and production, embodied in the ever more efficient state, fostered these frontiers and consumed the resources of the land. We have not comprehended fully the degree to which human society has relied on landed resources to undergird economic development. Those untouched lands and new frontiers are fast dwindling, but the social forces that have driven frontier expansion have abated little, if at all. Our states, markets and peoples search for, but will no longer find, new frontier lands. (177)

This is a point to which I shall be returning in §7.2.

A further point which needs making in this context is that we are wrong to think of ecological damage in terms of the modern boundaries of states, since ecological damage knows no boundaries and can spread from country to country. In any case the modern concept of 'Ethiopia' is a formalised expression of a much more fluid and subtle network of alliances, trading relationships, and interconnectednesses that was the pre-modern area of north-east Africa. Indeed the present boundaries of Ethiopia are those of empire of the Neguses Theodore and Menelek, carved out in the late nineteenth century, in imitation of the European colonial empires, and with European rifles. The recent independence of Eritrea, after a bloody civil war, indicates that such artificial constructions as the enlarged Ethiopia cannot sustain themselves indefinitely, and perhaps indicates that neither can the more ambitious constructions of modernity.

Moreover this explanation can also be used to answer a common objection to the notion of colonialist exploitation. 'Poor countries,' the argument goes, 'Are poor because they have no resources'. And this is true to a certain extent, many '3rd World' countries do have few resources, but when we remember that modernity has drawn the political map of the world then it becomes easier to see that part of the exploitation of a country is precisely this delineation of boundaries. The Sahel countries of Africa, for example, are desperately poor, but before modernity their people existed in a trading relationship with the west African coastal countries; this trade continues of course, but the attempted modernisation and re-orientation of the economies of these coastal countries also destroys the traditional trading relationships of the whole area and thus impoverishes at second hand.

In the remainder of this section I shall list briefly some of the major areas of concern.

1. Forest resources — tropical forests, at current rates of depletion will all be gone by 2050. The World Resources Institute records the almost unbelievable world statistic of 0.8% annual clearance of forest during the period 1981-90 (ie every year 0.8% of the acreage of the world's forest as at 1981 is cleared) (308). The clearance of temperate forests has apparently stabilised this century, and the

acreage of temperate forest may even have even increased. However we should remember that this figure conceals the widespread replacement of native forests with plantations, which are of very little real conservation value, and in many cases are worse, ecologically, than having no forests at all (conifer plantations in Scotland, for example, increase the acidification of streams and lakes). Moreover, as tropical forests are exhausted these temperate forests will come under renewed pressure. In particular the forest of Russia, some of the largest remaining areas of forest in the world, seem to be ripe for plunder.

As well as providing timber natural forests provide: fire-wood, food items (game and plant food), medicinal herbs, local and global climate regulation, water storage, space for 'swidden' agriculture, soil erosion protection, protection of species diversity &c &c.

2. Fish-stocks – along with trees, the fishes of the ocean have always been a potent symbol of the inexhaustibility of nature. However there is concern that stocks of fish all over the world are beginning to give out, and this is particularly worrying in view of the fact that fish is a good source of cheap protein for much of the world's population. Although fish stocks are known to crash and then recover unaccountably it cannot but be suspected that the main reason why these stocks are disappearing is the simple one of over-fishing, especially as all the world's fish-stocks appear to be decline at once; the World Resources Institute's latest report indicates that world-wide 29% more fish was caught in 1989-91 compared to 1979-81 (352). The recent dispute (early 1995) between Canada and Spain over fishing on the Newfoundland Banks has served to remind us of how the most unimaginably productive fishing grounds in the world a few hundred years ago, where, it was said, a man could have walked across the surface of the ocean on the backs of the cod, have been reduced to a figurative desert by thirty years of intensive fishing.

3. We have noted above that arable lands have increased by 466% in the last 300 years. However much of this expansion is in response to the degradation of existing arable land:

> Remembering that these estimates are controversial, we suggest that large fractions of the world's land surface have been damaged in such major ways as to be basically useless for agriculture (crops and livestock), constituting an area about the size of Africa. (Rozanov in Turner, 204)

Boris Rozanov goes on to point out that the annual loss of productive land through soil degradation is 30-35% more than at any time in the last 10,000 years. In the same volume Ian Douglas estimates that sediment transfer (ie eroded soil disappearing towards the ocean) has increased between 3 and 10 times since the 1920s (230).

4. In a similar way water is fast becoming a precious commodity. Mark L'Vovich suggests that as a result of greater uptake of water (35 times its seventeenth-century level) and as a result of greater evaporation from cleared land, aquifers world wide are becoming depleted (in Turner 245). The other side of the coin is that, as a result of over-irrigation, large areas of the world face the problem of salinisation of arable land.

6.7 As well as the degradation of natural resources we should also consider the levels of **pollution** in the environment. This is especially apt in view of the fact that now 'the human input to the basic chemical flows of the biosphere is on the same scale as the natural' (Clark and Matthews in Turner 140).

Pollution most often enters the news as one-off catastrophes such as the Exxon Valdes disaster in Alaska. But more troubling is the insidious build-up of pollution in every part of the biosphere. It affects water ('88% of industrial uptake of water world-wide is returned to the hydrosphere contaminated in one way or another' (L'Vovich in Turner, 245)) in every form and indeed one of the signal features of modernity is that it is now inadvisable to drink water from steams, or even to swim in natural bodies of water in most parts of the world. But this pollution also affects the air, the smogs of big cities are legendary, but it has wider implications than this. Research has shown that upland lakes in Europe, often hundreds of miles from industrial areas, have been acidified, and therefore made poorer, by air-borne pollution since the Industrial Revolution (Pearce 3). The contemporary problem of Acid Rain, and accompanying *Waldsterben* of Northern and Central Europe are part of the same problem.

Contamination of air, drinking water and foodstuffs by agricultural and industrial chemicals is yet another problem and, taken all together, this pollution is such that cancers, probably, as Thomas McKeown argues, all caused by environmental contaminants, are the major cause of death in modern developed societies. Another example of an increased incidence of disease caused by environmental pollution is asthma, which in Australia has increased fourfold since 1945. Better diagnosis may account for a part of this, as may the official explanation, that it is caused by an increase in house-dust (thanks to air-conditioned and sealed houses) and grass-pollen (thanks to clearance of woodland to produce pasture). However it would seem that a more polluted atmosphere is also a significant cause. When the greater incidence of disease attributable to environmental pollution and degradation will cancel out the gains in health from modern medicine and the apparatus of modern medical supervision is an interesting question to consider.

In developing countries, where pollution is undoubtedly worse (Clark and Matthews in Turner, 140), especially as these countries often function as the developed world's dustbin (Headrich in Turner, 65), its effect is masked by earlier deaths from other, more immediate causes, such as industrial accidents and malnutrition and epidemic diseases.

A further dimension to the problem of pollution is the frightening build-up of domestic and industrial refuse in developed and developing countries. A disposable nappy is assumed to take 2000 years to break down, for example, and many other standard household items are just as permanent.

6.8 **Population** is a difficult environmental problem to discuss briefly, despite the fact that it is the one every one knows about. The world's population is currently 5.67 billion and, if things continue as they are at present, it is set to rise to 7.92 billion by 2015 and 12.5 billion by 2050. If the measures adopted by the 1994 World Population Conference in Cairo are adopted the rise will only be to 7.27 billion by 2015 (UN figures). It is also thought that the world has a maximum capacity of about 12 billion, but only if all resources are distributed equally (currently the developed world consumes 80% of the world's resources).

One of the difficulties of dealing with this question is that, like environmental degradation (§6.4), population growth is never seen as a direct result of modernity's activities and even more than environmental degradation, it is something that other, usually black, people do, and their own fault. In fact what seems to have happened is that at around 1850, just as the population growth of the then developed countries was beginning to slow down, the rate of increase of the rest of the world began to rocket (Whitmore in Turner, 26-31). I would argue that it was modernity's creation of a global economic space which permitted the increase in population in the first place, just as modernity can influence environmental degradation at second-hand (§6.4).

For it is incontestable that population increases with modernisation. Thus in Britain the population rose from 7.7 million in 1790 to 13.3 million in 1830. However why this occurs is not often explained well. Pre-modern societies have usually managed to control population increase (overall the population has risen steadily throughout human history, but without the enormous increase in modernity the theoretical maximum for the planet would have been so far away as to be almost unimaginable — if human population had continued to grow at the pre-modern rate, it still would not have reached one billion).

Amongst writers who deal with this question there is often a dark rhetoric of the diseased and bloody history of human population; before the Industrial Revolution, we are to believe, an enormous percentage of infants died before adulthood, adults themselves scarcely had time to produce enormous families before succumbing themselves to disease and starvation, and there was widespread abortion and infanticide.

Even leaving aside difficult questions as, is a long life necessarily a good thing? (is it better to live for 40 years in excellent health, or to live 40 years in excellent health and another 30 with arthritis, for example?), and various cultures have had different views on this, it needs to be said that there every indication that pre-modern cultures usually managed their population, not by infanticide or abortion (very inefficient methods of population control), but by social customs of late marriage and sexual abstinence. The savage as a rampaging sexual beast is, as everyone knows, a construction of the western imagination. Humans are generally much less sexual than most people want to believe.

Modernisation effects an increase in population not by greater prosperity immediately lowering the infant mortality-rate (for that rate in fact increases in all newly-industrialised societies), but by bringing people together into large cities, where the neglect of traditional sanctions against early marriage, and the personal economic advantage of producing many future workers, combine to cause a massive leap in population. The enormous growth in the third-world rural population is thus a secondary phenomenon of modernity; indeed it is a mistake to look at any part of the world now as evidence of how pre-modern societies functioned, since what we see now is a partially modernised, and wholly disrupted, world.

Population seems to be, and this is saying a lot considering the other ecological concerns we have already detailed, one of the most intractable of all humanity's problems. Conventional wisdom suggests that increasing affluence means fewer children; but experience does not bear this out, and the end of population growth in, say nineteenth-century France, had nothing to do with some sort of general prosperity, which did not arrive until the second half of the next century (Whitmore in Turner, 26). There is no saying that in other countries the same slowing in population will occur. In any case, increasing the prosperity of the 5-6 billion current inhabitants of the world to 'Northern' levels, however desirable, is just not possible; as Gandhi put it 'If it took England the exploitation of half the globe to be what it is today, how many globes will it take India?' (quoted in Jacobs 1).

6.9 The same problem with the global cultural and actual space which modernity has created leads us to consider **AIDS/HIV**. At first sight it seems odd to think of AIDS/HIV as an environmental problem. Since it was recognised in the early 80s it has been treated as either a medical or a moral problem. But it is useful to consider it as the most obvious symptom of a wider problem, that of 'global market' in diseases, pests and introduced species.

Alfred Crosby, in his *Ecological Imperialism*, has argued that the most effective weapons of European conquerors have always been diseases and pests common and controllable in Europe, but devastating in newly-colonised lands. Currently the formerly separate parts of the world are unified in one economic and cultural sphere, which means that diseases and pests can be transferred, despite precautions, from one end of the earth to another, and there establish themselves. AIDS, for example, seems to have been a rare viral disease of western Africa until transported to the United States, sometime post-war, and thence re-exported to all parts of the world. The propaganda of certain countries, such as China and Vietnam, which at first depicted the disease as an exclusively western problem, can be dismissed as 'westerner-bashing'. But it has an element of truth in it, when we remember that AIDS did enter these countries initially as a result of infected westerners.

Moreover there is nothing to suggest that, bad as AIDS is, that virus, or another, could not develop into an even worse disease. It is also surprising that since the great Flu Epidemic of 1919 the strains of flu which have been circulating have been relatively mild ones; there is nothing to suggest that this will not alter in the future either.

In other words the global biological arena which modernity has created is the area in which, not only capital, but diseases and pests can circulate, to everyone's disadvantage.

6.10 The final area of concern I want to address here is the **depletion of biological diversity**. Partly as a result of global biological sphere which modernity has created (§6.9), which allows pests, introduced plants and feral animals to invade every ecosystem on the planet, and partly as a result of deliberate destruction, the number of species of animals and plants becoming extinct or endangered is large and growing every day.

Animal species should not be allowed to become extinct because this disrupts natural food-chains and causes environmental disruption. For example the general massacre of birds of prey in England by game-keepers in the nineteenth-century resulted in much increased levels of crop-damage by sparrows, pigeons and starlings. Plant species should not be allowed to die out for the same reasons, and because they might well prove to be useful, as food or medicinal plants, or as useful sources of materials. But no plant or animal species can be protected on its own, but only within its natural habitat, and the number and diversity of animal species within a given habitat is a useful indicator of the ecological health of the environment.

I will be arguing later in the book that the cognate reduction of *cultural* diversity is a significant problem for humanity too (§7.2).

6.11 The foregoing sections should, perhaps be allowed to speak for themselves, beyond pointing out that the 'Ecological Crisis' is indeed a crisis in the traditional

MAGDALEN COLLEGE LIBRARY

sense, but by no means a crisis in the newer sense (§6.1). However there are five additional points to be borne in mind.

1. That modernity, as we have seen, is the same system, with the same dynamics, throughout its history; only the *scale* of its operations changes, and the greater the scale the greater the environmental destructiveness:

> Most global-scale impacts of human-induced changes have been recent, particularly those dealing with [sic] the biogeochemical flows of the biosphere. Only a few of the components of the biosphere ... attained 50% of their current level of change before the twentieth century, and probably the majority attained this level around or after the mid-point of the century. (Turner 13)

Moreover, nothing indicates that this relentless drive to consume all has generally abated at all, although in a few areas some reduction in the acceleration of destruction may be noticeable. We should not be misled by cosmetic changes, such as the phasing-out of CFCs in the developed world, or the discontinuation of the use of mercury in batteries. The real problem is the *scale* of modernity's economic activity, which will not, and cannot, be reduced. As has been remarked, it's good to recycle paper, and preferable to using more wood-pulp, water and energy, but recycling paper uses energy and water, and often other resources, so it would be better to reduce consumption of paper in the first place.

2. There is often a paucity of data about the extent of environmental destruction, and so all the more controversy about its significance. It is quite easy to see that as information, like everything else, is bought and sold, there should be plenty of information produced indicating little cause for concern, indeed we would expect it, as science, as we noted above (§6.2) is ideologically neutral and can be used as a tool by either conservationists or modernity's vested interests equally. (Thus science can either be a useful way of creating low-cost, low-technology, low-energy processes and equipment, locally produced and locally consumed, or expensive, sophisticated, high-energy processes and equipment for mass-production and mass consumption.) Conversely there is often little data on questions of no immediate economic significance (Clark and Matthews in Turner, 139). For example, the world-wide loss of humus from soils, as a result of over-cropping and bad management, is (presumably) large, but completely unquantifiable (Rozanov in Turner 212).

3. One thought that arises in considering the above point is that the world environment, or indeed any part of it, is a vastly complex system and, although as children of a paradigm which exalts positivistic science we would be loath to give way to irrationality, yet the idea of ever truly understanding all the elements that enter into the environment and the causal effects they produce is a strongly hubristic one. Perhaps what we ought to think in terms of is a simple drawing back, in a

humble recognition of our ignorance, and a return to a state where the environment was not pushed to its limits. In pre-modern times most cultures (Europe being the exception) contrived always to have a large ecological safety-net for their activities. Thus in many accounts written by early European explorers of other parts of the world we find accounts of the enormous abundance of birds, animals, fish, forest-tracts &c—all indicators of the wise husbandry of the indigenes. A more rational view of human achievement might see the agricultural cultures of New Guinea, many of which have persisted for more than 10,000 years without any significant environmental degradation, as more worthy of praise than the costly and as yet short-lived triumphs of modernity (given enough resources and energy anybody can do anything, the really neat trick is to do something with nothing).

4. Although I have tried to separate the various elements of the ecological crisis and to give a short but accurate summary of the latest wisdom on them, as yet none of the various elements are well-enough studied to be predictable, and most also contain positive-feedback mechanisms within themselves (§6.4). Moreover rarely is one element the whole extent of the problem for '[environmental] problems are now beginning to compound themselves interactively in ways which challenge even near term predictions' (McAdams in Turner, ix).

5. All the environmental concerns we have documented have as their fundamental basis the expansion of the economic sphere of modernity beyond safe bounds. Although we have seen that, owing to the complex overlay of prior temporalities by a modernistic temporality, modernity cannot be held *directly* responsible for every act of environmental degradation which has or is occurring (§6.4) yet it is not difficult to see what, in the last instance, is causing this degradation:

> Apart from fairly localized areas of siltation, alluviation, and downcutting, and from patches of salinization and some fairly extensive areas of deforestation that were at least partly reversible ... [environmental] impacts were few and essentially negligible before the Industrial Revolution. (McAdams in Turner, ix)

It should also be noted that it doesn't actually matter what depth of time we attribute the degradation of natural resources, since the problem is here and has to be faced. However, Europe is a very bad and atypical example of human societies, which have usually managed to practise a better husbandry. Moreover the expansion of Europe from c.1450 onwards should be seem not as a sign of Europe's greater dynamism, but of Europe's greater desperation in seeking to evade the consequences of its ecological unsustainability.

Above all modernistic, 'high-tech' solutions cannot solve the basic problem of environmental degradation, which is the *size* of modernity's economic sphere.

6.12 A final point to make in this chapter is concerned with the concept of 'nature'. Nature and the protection of the natural world have often been either the starting-point or the focus of oppositional activity and it isone of the most urgent tasks facing a movement oppositional to modernity is to safeguard natural resources from the greedy ravages of industry.

However there is a danger in dwelling too much upon the concept of 'nature' as understood in traditional liberal discourses, and especially on the related concept of 'wilderness'. We should remember that:

> Every hectare from the Arctic to the Antarctic is owned, demarcated, and con-trolled. Every hectare of land is subject to the formally recognised ownership and control of an individual, an organisation, or a nation-state. Primaeval wilderness—in the sense of untrodden forests or deserts—exists only in our collective imagination. In the late 1980s the land and its wealth is subject to human management. The earth is now at our disposal. (Richards in Turner 162).

And indeed this is not a new phenomenon, almost all of what we traditionally regard as 'wild nature' has been profoundly affected by human action. And this is not true only of such areas as the British Isles, the natural habitats of which, as Oliver Rackham has recently shown in his *History of the Countryside*, are all the result of human influence on natural habitats and resources, but also of such areas as Australia. Here the European view of the land as 'natural' and of the Aborigines as living at the mercy of the elements has had to be modified recently as more and more evidence comes to light of the profound influence which the indigenous inhabitants had upon the vegetation of every part of the continent.

What the liberal view of a dichotomy between human landscapes and wilderness does is to reinforce the idea that certain bits of the landscape (usually a long car-drive or plane-trip away) are inviolable, but that the rest of the environment is up for grabs. Wilderness then becomes the preserve of eco-tourism, often to the detriment of the indigenous people of the area, who, in this view, are simply a nuisance and an anomaly (unless they can be persuaded to become tour-guides), and everywhere else is ripe for development.

A development of this view is that a price can be put on the environment. This is a particularly marked feature of a certain brand of green economics. This approach to the problem of environmental degradation is useful for persuading government and business that parts of the environment are valuable and that traditionally the environmental costs of any particular enterprise have not been paid. But apart from this approach seems to be very worrying. For what the effect of this process is to reduce everything to the same kind of commodity, so that it can be traded on the global market. For it is clear that different things and different resources should have different uses (no one, for example, would buy a painting by Titian, put legs on it and use it as a dining table). Yet when a 'price' is set upon a piece of real estate or on the environment generally (in the form of a pollution tax, for example) then what is being offered is the opportunity to destroy that habitat by building on it, or to damage the environment by polluting, as the pollution tax or the environmental levy is unlikely to be high enough to prevent the destruction or pollution taking place; the desired outcome is really not to have the habitat destroyed or any pollution in the environment.

This is not the same argument as saying, as a liberal view would have it, that wilderness is priceless. What it is saying is that it doesn't matter what price is set on a piece of desirable real estate, if it enters the modernistic sphere of development it will be destroyed utterly. The only solution is not to quibble about how much it is worth, but to think about contesting development *per se*. Indeed liberal environmentalism always neglects, for example, very damaged habitats or urban landscapes, but in truth, everywhere is sacred and nowhere should be allowed to be developed in the modernistic sense. Thus the 'Nimby' ['Not In My BackYard'] mentality of liberal environmentalism must be taken a stage further, for everywhere is somebody's backyard.

A further problem with liberal environmentalism, *and this applies also to the gains of liberalism in terms of social justice*, is that there is no guarantee that these gains cannot be reversed in the future. National Parks, Nature Reserves, environmental protection legislation seem inviolable, yet there is nothing to say that when the times get tough these will not just be rescinded. Social justice provisions worldwide have been scaled back in late capitalism and same also applies to specific nature conservation measures. It is a frightening thought that all the damage that has been caused by modernity around the world has been when the going was good — what sort of fanatical desperation will modernity call up when the going gets harder?

A final point to make here is that my views on cultural relativity entail a view of the world which sees natural phenomena as only having any meaning when mediated through human culture. There is no nature, only various views of the natural world. This might seem at first sight to offer no protection to any part of the world, as modernity, as we've seen, refuses to recognise any area of the world as unavailable for development, often not even 'wilderness'. On the other hand modernity is, as I've argued, on a short trip to nowhere, and, whether modified or not, will soon end. Moreover environmentalists from almost the beginning of modernity have pointed out the environmental short-comings of modernity; so, in reality no one can be excused for falling into a modernistic view of nature as being up for grabs.

The view of nature attaining meaning only through human mediation, is in fact a profoundly comforting one. For it allows the possibility of the emergence of a paradigm of belief characterised by the recognition that human cultures are only ever long-lasting or sustainable when they recognise that humans are not set apart from nature, but are always humans-in-nature. As Yirawala, the Gunwinggu ceremonial leader, artist and land-rights activist put it: 'Money is like water that flows away, but the land is for ever'. And Sandra Le Brun Holmes book about him makes it clear that for the Gunwinggu people of Arnhem Land in northern Australia there was no dichotomy between humans and nature, or human landscapes and wilderness, but all humans are of nature and all areas are at once everyday and sacred.

There is a strain of environmental thought which sees humans as a disease and a blight on the world. According to this view the world was a beautiful place until humans came along and ruined everything. Now this view is hardly ever articulated like this, because its fatuousness would at once be apparent, but the implications of this view are allowed to linger and when they do so they are inclined to give credence, ironically enough, to all-out modernistic development, for, the train-of-thought goes, if we are unnatural, a disease, a pest, then why do we not simply do our worst, since whatever we do tends to increase entropy in the environment.

The view I should like to oppose to this is that it does matter very much what kinds of interactions we carry out with the natural world, since we can either carry out those which lead to widespread degradation and disruption (as in modernity), or local, small-scale interactions which may in fact increase the ecological diversity of the environment (for example traditional water-meadows in the south of England are not natural, but the result of human construction for the purposes of livestock feeding — nevertheless they are refuges for rare and unusual animals and plants, such as the Fritillary (*Fritillaria meleagris*)).

As to the charge we are not 'natural', this is simply a reflection of the often-described western 'unhappiness in the world' that seems to have begun when Augustine invented the doctrine of Original Sin. Every species has some sort of effect on its environment and humans are no exception. The only difference is that humans can think and can try to predict whether the changes they make to their environment are in the interests of their species. Indeed environmentalism is emphatically not a spirituality, or a moral cause, it is naked self-interest — modernistic development, on the hand, is the worst kind of spirituality.

Chapter Seven:
Capitalism Out of Control

7.1 In the last chapter I argued that the capitalistic temporality of modernity is ecologically unsustainable in the long term. And earlier I argued that a strange feature of modernity is the way it gives every appearance of being rational and conservative, whilst in fact it is not only radical and disruptive, but completely divorced from almost anything that had gone before in human history (§1.2). We also saw earlier that an understanding of cultural relativity prevents us from making substantive criticisms of other cultures and from condemning wholesale our own culture (§3.5). However there is an obvious exception: if we find on examination that a particular culture cannot maintain itself in the long term, then we are entitled to condemn it, as failing to fulfil the only 'morality' any culture ever has, that of ensuring its own continuation. Indeed we can say that only with modernity does humanity become enough of a general danger to itself to be worth taking seriously.

Thus we can say that, in common with other societies modernity suffers from the 'cultural delusion' (Bellett 34), that it knows and is exercising the correct solution to its ecological problems. This notion must be contested by every means possible.

7.2 But worse than this, capitalistic modernity has the effect of so reducing cultural diversity that the cultural flexibility that is necessary for the oncoming age of ecological uncertainty and rapid change is severely impaired. Throughout history various civilisations have had similar trajectories to modernity, although their cultural spaces have always been more restricted. Thus, for example, the ancient civilisations of Egypt and Mesopotamia and, more recently, China, have all shown rapid rises to extreme sophistication and then a period of very rapid collapse, recovery and collapse again (Whitmore in Turner, 26-31). It is ironic that these cultures have always been labelled 'great civilisations' when their entire history is one of giddy and short-lived prosperity followed by chaos and societal upheaval. Perhaps it is not difficult to understand why modernity regards these 'civilisations' as such, as they are so similar in pattern to modernity itself. Really long-term sustainability of culture is shown only by those societies which, one way or another, contrive always to have some sort of spare environmental resources at hand, as, for instance in the famous case of the 40,000+ year history of the Australian Aborigines. We might explain the instability of the 'great civilisations', on the other hand, as the result of these civilisations expanding and then running out of frontiers (§6.6).

Modernity of course does not possess this reserve, and has made sure, by appropriation, that nobody else possesses any either. Thus there are two faces to the problem. The first is that modernity itself, through its over-specialisation and its reliance on energy-hungry technology is inflexible:

> Today humanity faces a difficult ... situation. First, the drives towards gratification and predictable control (order) are more strongly institutionalized than ever before. Second, modern institutional forms, while offering great productive capacity, are more rigid and vulnerable to failure when overstressed than traditional institutions. Third, modern institutions systematically neglect or obscure larger changes in the natural environment—in part because, conceptually, nature increasingly has been absorbed into industrial culture. (Bennett in Turner, 71, see also Handmer)

But the other part of the problem is that capitalistic modernity has replaced or overshadowed other cultural systems, which might offer other possibilities for a more long-term future for human societies. Cultural diversity is just as important as biological diversity for the survival of humanity but it has been almost wholly neglected. If we were logically consistent, alongside programmes to eradicate rats, cats and other pests from tropical islands, we would run programmes to eliminate capitalism from these same habitats. Indeed the well-meaning efforts of aid and international agencies are often as effective as the most crass acts of economic imperialism in bringing traditional societies 'into the modern world'. One thinks of Joan Robinson's jibe at 'foreign experts' who turn up in a country 'telling people what they ought to want' (xi).

It is worth spending time here outlining briefly the reasons why cultural diversity is desirable, since the case is not often argued to its logical conclusion.

Although humans do still evolve genetically modernity has not yet found a way to influence this (although it is conceivable that radiation or pollution, or some sort of revived eugenics in the guise of 'genetic engineering', may do this in the future). However humans also evolve *culturally* in the much shorter term and cultures can fulfil the same role in cultural history as populations do in genetic evolution.

Now to us westerners it is an *a priori* that we are the best equipped to deal with any future ecological changes (this despite the fact that it is our culture that caused most of the changes in the first place). But this is by no means the case: we are still crucially dependent on agriculture, and our agriculture is dependent on modern plant-breeding (and therefore the social institution of scientific research), oil and oil products, agricultural chemicals, and fertilisers. Now all of these are dependent on the continuance of the global economic system, if any one of the above were to be threatened, then our entire agricultural system would be placed in jeopardy. In fact the only thing that modern agriculture has going for it is the enormous weight of capital propping it up. (An allegory for modernistic agriculture would be someone who walked back and forth over Niagara Falls on a tightrope, and claimed that not only was it perfectly safe, but that everyone should be made to cross by this method).

In contrast the traditional farmer with his tiny plot of land, his miserable yields and his labour-intensive farm is rather pitiful. But there is no sense in which we can judge the traditional farmer to be in a worse position. On balance, his position is the better one, since his crops are diversified and suited to local conditions, not requiring chemical fertilisers or herbicides and insecticides, and his locale (ideally) has a sufficient ecological safety margin. However it is the case that since the Green Revolution (§1.5) modernity has increasingly marginalised traditional agriculture, when it should be obvious that it would have been better to preserve as many and as varied traditional agricultures as possible.

Another point to be made here is that the traditional view of 'primitive' societies being 'at the mercy of nature' needs to be stood on its head. In the centuries of European expansion throughout the world no trope was more prominent in explorers' accounts than that of 'miserable savages at the mercy of nature'. And yet this is clearly an absurd proposition. Any society has to work with the resources to hand, but if any such group truly is very vulnerable to the vicissitudes of the environment (climate, food supply, natural disasters &c) then clearly it would have died out at some stage. That European explorers 'discovered' that every corner of the world, except Antarctica, was populated proves that, although local extinctions may have occurred, they are not very common. Also, at some stage of human history the ancestors of the Europeans must also have been 'at the mercy of the elements', and yet, clearly they did not die out.

In fact it needs pointing out that although life is generally harder and shorter in a society which is not extended, or technologically 'advanced', such societies are actually less at risk of general disaster and mortality than modern societies, since it is only in modernity that the techniques of killing people by the thousand and the million have been perfected, as, for example, the 'mere' 40,000 civilians

MAGDALEN COLLEGE LIBRARY

killed recently in an 'internal police operation' in Chechnya. Moreover the scale of modernity's economic activities is such that any disaster produces fatalities and injuries far beyond any possible natural disaster could produce in smaller scale societies. This vulnerability is masked by the excellent disaster-relief and emergency services provided by many developed nations, but there is no guarantee that in the future such services will remain intact and functioning. It would be interesting to try to compile figures of fatalities and deaths attributable to modernistic development from its beginnings: they would not be modest.

A further point to make in this context, though concerning cultural diversity in the widest sense, is that women do very badly in modernity, because they are expected to take their part in the one societal economic system *and* fulfil more traditional roles such as child-rearing and house-work. In other societies, though women are often not as highly valued as men (this is one of the most notable 'family resemblances' (§3.5) of cultures), they have several spheres, or temporalities, in which to operate, so their marginalisation can at least be palliated. In modernity there are no 'women's spaces' or spheres, only the one work-force. Is it not the case that a society which so marginalises what is effectively the majority of its members is less efficient than one that allows more scope to women? Here, as elsewhere, modernity's peculiar genius is to reduce everything to the extreme case, and push everything to breaking point.

7.3 Thus, in one sense, capitalism is 'out of control'. But it is out of control in another sense too, insofar as capitalistic modernity's global reach means that nation-states, except the very largest, are often powerless to counteract the effects of modernity, even when these have undeniable and profound consequences for the domestic economies of these nations.

On the one hand this is not necessarily a cause for lamentation as nation-states themselves are often simply products of an earlier phase of modernity. Many, for example, are artificial creations of post-colonial times, such as many African nations, which are a complete nonsense in any cultural or historical sense and long-overdue for dissolution. In other parts of the world the imposition of modern notions of the state is at variance with the actual history of the region, so that, for instance in China, the idea of modern state, perhaps more than communism, has led this century to a cruel and sudden sinification of areas which were only ever nominally part of China, and certainly not Chinese in culture, as for example, Manchuria, Inner Mongolia, Sinkiang, Tibet and parts of the south.

On the other hand some nations are reasonably authentic and legitimate cultural units (eg Denmark) and it is a shame to see them buffeted hither and thither by the vagaries of international capitalism.

7.4 I should like to illustrate briefly those agents of international capitalism, as with my list of ecological concerns in chapter six, this list is illustrative, not necessarily exhaustive or authoritative:

1. Most notable is the push for international Free Trade via the Gatt agreements. Although global Free Trade is a chimera, a thing to be aspired to, rather than a realistic goal and as often as not contradicted by other things that the developed nations of the world do (see point 2) it is none the less a symbolic demonstration of modernity's aspirations. And whatever is done in the way of lowering barriers and tariffs is usually very economically damaging to one or other of the trading partners, and often both. Thanks to global Free Trade the indigenous people of South America can have the privilege of watching their forests being cleared for cattle-grazing, the poor quality meat produced going largely to the US pet-meat trade (Williams in Turner, 191). Such benefits of Free Trade are not confined to this particular case, but are widely afforded by developed nations to less developed ones.

2. As a result of the infinitely deferred nature of the establishment of global Free Trade regional trading blocks are now springing up all round the world. Occasionally there are benefits, as when European Community regulations force a recalcitrant British government to introduce some limited measures of social justice. Otherwise, however, these trading blocs are rather like neighbourhood watch schemes, with each country now kept even more firmly on the economic straight and narrow by the increased scrutiny of and economic intercourse with its neighbours.

3. The case of multinational companies is well known. Many such enterprises are economically larger than small nation states and have corresponding power. Furthermore, by operating in several countries international companies can locate each of its subsidiary parts in the most advantageous situation and can avoid scrutiny of the totality of its operations.

There has been some suggestion that in future the business world will not be dominated by these giants, but by smaller and local enterprises. But such evidence of this as has been produced indicates rather that international companies are now wise to the disrepute they enjoy and have taken care to diversify in name and in structure, whilst maintaining overall direction and strategy. Even where their organisations have been broken down completely the various constituant parts of the organisation can be trusted to operate with an uncanny kind of telepathy, so that the end result is the same as if the organisation had not been broken down. Enviromentalists and other political activists are often big on conspiracy theories (that big business is out to get them, that the defence establishment is behind eveything), but the truth is usually that no conspiracy is

71

needed, but the subjects of modernity, so true children of modernity are they, simply act 'naturally' and the end result is just as if they had colluded.

A further point to make here is that international business is not only damaging in itself, but is the agent of dissemination of western tastes and desires. Thus there are several well-known international fast-food companies, but these also spawn a host of local competitors and encourage the same sort of behaviour on the part of local concerns as they themselves demonstrate world-wide.

4. As is well-known there now exists a global information and entertainment network. Thus, for example, international news media can beam their programmes across national borders, providing information where previously little had existed. The international media have been widely praised for bringing about several anti-communist revolutions in Eastern Europe, but it is fair to say that the international media will never bring about an anti-capitalist revolution anywhere: how could they, as their programmes are designedly instruments to create new markets for their advertisers' goods and to disseminate 'democratic' (ie modernistic) values?

5. A final agent of the internationalisation of modernity is the international currency market, at once the most impressive and the most bathetic of modernity's institutions. Like everything about modernity it claims a natural status, but in fact its history is recent and inglorious; it simply emerged after the relaxation of currency controls in the 70s and early 80s.

This market trades currencies, and every day its turnover is larger than the *annual* turnover of most countries' economies, trillions of dollars a year. No national government can influence it directly and it is often immune from any action such governments take, as when the £ sterling fell (or was it pushed?) in September 1992, despite the millions of pounds the British Treasury spent on trying to keep it at a higher level. Smaller currencies, such as the $Australian, which really have no business at all to be traded, are often pushed about in a less dramatic, but more peremptory manner, and this influences the domestic economic policy of these countries to an even greater extent.

Just like modernity as a whole the International Money Market is on the largest scale, but locally its effects are always destructive and cannot, by their very nature, be anything otherwise.

7.5 However, modernity is 'out of control' in yet a third way. In §7.1 and 7.2 I argued that one of the problems with modernity was that, not only was it unsustainable in itself, but it has the property of preventing other cultures from exercising ecological prudence. But, if as I have argued earlier our model is not the crude domination of one culture by another, but the superimposition of a capitalistic temporality on prior temporalities (§1.3), then problems are created for this view. For really what we are seeing is not the collision of cultures, but the contestation of temporalities *across* cultures. In other words, in the past cultures were more autonomous and more homogenous, mostly because they were geographically more isolated, but nowadys the global reach of modernity has affected all cultures, though obviously not to the same extent in each context.

For the power of modernity to effect transcultural influence is attributable to its single-minded concentration on the market. Every known human society has had or has some sort of arrangement whereby goods are traded. But every other human society has, not a market, but *markets*, that is, not everything is reduced to the same kind of commodity, but different goods are sold or bartered in different markets, in different circumstances and with particular customs and expectations. The switch to a capitalist temporality is thus not so alien, simply the replacement of a complex situation with a very dull, literal-minded one.

Just as I argued that it is a cause for hope that pre-modern temporalities can persist within modernity (§1.4) so it is a similar cause for hope that in societies only recently influenced by modernity, if modernity's influence were to be abated, then the market might swing back to an economy of traditional markets. For it is to be observed that where capitalist production has only just begun it is often not truly capitalist in that there is no emphasis on developing revolutions in production (§1.2), but simply of cashing in on the present advantages (low wages, non-unionised labour). Such set-ups are often no more than a productive organisation of traditional injustices backed up by traditional methods of coercion. There is certainly no attempt in these cases to create a quiescent and pliable middle-class.

However, other societies, notably those of east Asian states of neo-Confucian statist culture, Japan, South Korea, Taiwan, Singapore and China, have adopted capitalism more enthusiastically, and have become more modernistic in some respects than the traditional core-states of modernity (Britain, Germany, France, USA &c). In this respect then modernity is no longer even 'our' (ie western) problem exclusively.

In addition we now are beginning to see that other developing countries are using the weapons of modernity's own propaganda to argue against any reining in of the excesses of modernity. The Prime Minister of Malaysia, for example, has repeatedly said that western concern over tropical forest destruction and other ecological damage occurring in Malaysia is simply a neo-colonialist attempt to prevent Malaysia developing its economy. The West, Dr Mohathir adds, must pay if they want to see tropical forests in Malaysia preserved.

This, besides being an almost unassailable rhetoric position, has an element of truth in it. For if modernity is based on the liberal notion of the

MAGDALEN COLLEGE LIBRARY

individual (chapter three), and concerned with the development of that individual's true (modernistic) personality, then modernity needs must be unfair, discriminatory and racist, for the one thing which the developed world *cannot* allow is for all the world's inhabitants to enjoy the same individuality (in material terms) as the citizens (or certain of them) of the developed world. I would agree with the Malaysian Prime Minister that the west should pay for environmental protection in the rest of colonised world, but the form I shall suggest this should take is perhaps not what he had in mind (§9.2.4).

7.6 The final point which needs to be made in this context, and one related to the foregoing point, is that there can be no easy or quick return to pre-modern conditions, even if an immediate end to modernity is possible. For the history of modernity and western colonisation generally has been to disarrange nearly all the chaotic, but chaotically stable and fantastically intricate ethnic and cultural relations around the pre-modern world. (For examples of pre-modern diversity and complexity think of the strange and archaic settlement patterns in Greece and Asia Minor as revealed in the Greek historians from Herodotus to Pausanias; for a modern example think of the more than 600 languages of the various cultural groups on the island of New Guinea). Everywhere in the world we see colonised and super- and juxtaposed societies, settler colonies, populations of former slaves or indentured workers or *Gastarbeiter*. Few of these societies have very harmonious relations, few countries in the world are wholly untouched by these modern diasporas, and fewer still are in their authentic pre-modern state. Any possible end of modernity will have to see any number of negotiations and complex settlements in these situations.

A further caveat is that as modernity has had such a profound effect on every part of the world the assertion of pre-modern authenticity, although a powerful rhetorical tool, is an unhelpful and disingenuous one. Except in a very few cases no group or society can claim to be wholly authentic, and a major part of the work of praeter-modernity will be the refabrication of authenticities.

Chapter Eight:
Opposition

8.1 In the chapters six and seven I described how modernity is ecologically unsustainable and a danger to the cultural diversity of the world. For these two reasons opposition to modernity is necessary, moreover opposition must not simply be to certain aspects of modernity, but to one of the fundamental underpinnings of modernity, namely its global reach.

Thus anyone who accepts the premises and the arguments of this book so far cannot, by definition, be either a Marxist or a liberal critic of modernity, since both liberals and Marxists accept those very aspects of modernity which are most in question when we consider modernity's unsustainability and cultural imperialism. 'Let us leave to their pieties', as Foucault said in a different context those who believe that the market can solve the problems created by the market; the remainder of the book will hold nothing of interest for them, though the course of political action outlined in chapter nine is designed not to offend such sensibilities too much (cf §8.4.1-2).

The principal reason why opposition to modernity must be total and not based on any prevailing notions of opposition is that cultural systems always understand new ideas in terms of older ones. For example 'sustainable development' was originally a powerful concept put forward by green economists to define the sort of economic activity which would not prejudice the environment any further, and might even improve it. Recently however, as Sharon Beder has argued, the term has become a meaningless one through appropriation. Now, if it means anything at all, it means 'modernistic development which can be sustained' (a fine tautology). We might also like to think of how adjectives such as 'biodegradable', 'environmentally friendly' are now part of the rhetoric of advertising and selling, particularly of domestic products.

But two questions remain to be answered, firstly where will this opposition emanate from? and secondly, what concrete policies will it endorse?

MAGDALEN COLLEGE LIBRARY

8.2 It is in fact very difficult to imagine a possible future political coalition emerging in developed countries for the following reasons:
1. Green parties have been active since the 1970s in most developed countries; admittedly this is a rather short time, but during this period they have found that there seems to be a limit to the percentage of votes they can secure, of around 20%. Beyond this there seems to exist extreme opposition to green parties, politics and policies. As David Lowenthal puts it: 'People prefer to be gradually poisoned by industry than rapidly starved by the lack of it' (in Turner 132); or perhaps we should add more accurately 'than to run the apparent risk of starving without it'.

However, aside from this, there is a genuine reason why the middle-class voter *should* fear the Greens. In a recent Australian election a bumper-sticker appeared reading 'Greens Cost Jobs', the Greens immediately countered with a sticker reading 'Greens Boost Jobs', but in a way the first sticker was correct. It is true that green policies, and the policies advocated in chapter nine, would create jobs in a certain sense, but they would also take away the function of a job as cultural capital in a late capitalist world. Green policies would doubtless hit 'living standards' (as the term is widely understood), but worse they would hurt the pride and prestige of bourgeois wage-earners, by making work, rather than employment, once again simply a fact of life, not a privilege.
2. For we must not imagine that a green policies could ever be in the short-term interest of the middle-classes. Indeed there is a sociological theory that most of the support for green politics comes from people whose background is middle class/ professional, but who have been denied advancement in the professions by the rigours of late capitalism (Birrell 6). The 'rump' of the middle classes, those still enjoying a 'traditional' bourgeois life-style, have all the more reason to be tenacious of their privileges, when they see so many of their peers falling by the wayside.

And history has shown that the middle-classes have been very wary of any perceived threat to their living standards. In the 1930s slump, when capitalism came very close to collapse, the middle-classes rallied behind 'sound money' politics (the National Government of Ramsey MacDonald in Britain, a similar coalition government in Australia, led by Lyons). In Germany they turned to Nazism. In the 1970s and 80s, a similar time of crisis, governments dedicated to monetaristic policies and 'restructuring' were elected in Britain, the USA, Australia, Canada, France &c &c.

Indeed what else can the middle-classes do but hang on and hope for the best? it is inconceivable that in the short-term any such a large social group in any country of the world could enjoy so affluent a life-style. It would be naive to point out, for example, that absolute wealth has never been a good way of establishing preeminence as there is always someone wealthier, it is more a question of *relative* wealth. However it is not a question here of enumerating the superfluities that the middle-classes will have to give up (as for example does F.E.Trainer 29-33); simply of pointing out that 'life-styles' will have to curtailed in some way or another.

One thing, incidentally, that always amuses me is the way in which green politicians and political activists are depicted by the main-stream of the media as trouble-makers, intent on disrupting the lawful concerns of citizens. In doing this they draw upon the distinction, first articulated by Spinoza, of the civil society versus the prophetic order. In Spinoza's case civil society was the non-ideological, liberal society of freedom and philosophical inquiry which he longed for and the prophetic order the bigoted, hysterical, demagogic Calvinist political system of the late seventeenth-century Netherlands in which he lived. The main-stream media depiction of the greens in the present day leans on this distinction, modernity is seen as free, open, containing a host of possibilities and the greens seen as puritanical, hysterical terrorists, intent on destroying living standards out of sheer misanthropy. A moment's thought will show that Spinoza's ideal civil society has never, in fact, emerged and that modernity is a plausible successor to the Calvinistic hooliganry of his time. It is in fact modernity which is the prophetic order, and the modernistic temporality is one which owes a great deal to protestant thinking; whether a green civil society will emerge to contest modernity is doubtful, but it is certainly not the greens who are to blame for the ecological and political problems of the modern world. By the same token right-wing parties like the British Conservatives, or the Australian Liberal and National Parties, call themselves 'conservatives' whereas in fact they are the most radical and disruptive of political forces – the last real conservative in British politics was the Duke of Wellington, anyone subsequently claiming the title is an imposter, 'a damned Whig, a damned bad hat', as the Duke might have said.

At the same time, however, we should recognise that this perverse conservatism is nothing more than the, dare I say it?, natural habit of mind of any social group in the centre of power in any society; and indeed, were the paradigm we are in not modernity, then such an attitude might be more understandable, perhaps even admirable.

3. Nor should we hope for the revolution of the proletariat. For we have that even if this should occur, then all that will happen is that growth-economics will continue under a Marxist regime (chapter four). And in any case by late capitalism the working-classes have been so sapped in their political strength by *embourgeoisement* and marginalisation that their political power is effectively nil. In 'good times' unions are the cat's paw of capitalistic enterprise, as

MAGDALEN COLLEGE LIBRARY

Joan Robinson put it in the 1960s: 'the organisation of workers instead of over-throwing capitalism has been the means of keeping it going' (68). In bad times such organisations lose all their strength as their membership declines through unemployment.

4. Our education system is no more to be relied on to produce opposition than any other sector of society, since it does not represent an independent force which can comment on and influence society, but is simply one aspect of that society. Note for example how the provision of widely-available education in tied into the various stages of capitalism: primary education in early capitalism, to provide an educated and quiescent work-force; secondary in middle-capitalism, to widen the 'mass market' and to bring more of the middle-classes on board, and now in late capitalism tertiary education is being pushed more and more, as a way of reducing the workforce and disguising the unemployment figures, and as a response to the perceived need for training.

Just as it is not surprising that the middle-classes are conservative, rather to be expected, so it is that the idea of 'radical education' is a non-starter, as institution which is spread throughout society must be made so bland and unthreatening to the majority of its users that it cannot espouse very much in the way of radical culture. The current increase in ecological and environmental education in schools is to be welcomed, and it will remain to be seen what long-term effect this will have. However, I suspect that such an education will not, indeed cannot, within modernity, challenge the 'economic imperative', which, though not taught explicitly, doesn't have to be, since it is the air we breathe, the water we drink.

Higher education, particularly the humanities, has long been a famous preserve of so-called radicals; but the very small effect they have had on anything points both to the fact that, as Bourdieu has noted, radical academics are simply part of bourgeoisie which espouses a rhetoric of opposition, and to the fact that academia is no haven for non-modernistic ideas. One reason for this is that academic success is governed by peer-review, in other words the academics who get on are those who sound most like other academics and do not represent a threat to them or anyone. Another is that academics are generally ground down by the pressure of a 'sausage-factory' teaching schedule, and the daily practice of simplifying knowledge till it approximates to a liberal world-view, for bored and mutinous students (who was it who said 'almost everything taught in schools and universities is wrong'?). This is not a particular feature of late capitalism, though the admirers of the Keynesian dispensation would like to think it is (§2.5), but has always been the case. Of all academics biologists and ecologists are the most likely to be unfazed by modernistic rhetoric, since they have daily contact with the ecological imprudence of modernity — however the lure of research grants and consultancies for big companies often leads them astray too.

Incidentally this book is not an academic work, as it crosses so many disciplinary boundaries, and fails to respect the individual aesthetics of each separate discipline, as represented in modernity — therefore any academics who may be reading can feel perfectly justified in ignoring what they read as the work of a shaggy and impudent interloper.

5. Some people in modernity assert that a major strength of this paradigm is the bureaucratic apparatus of governmental supervision and control which surrounds, and indeed may constitute, the subjects of modernity. While it is true that it is this apparatus which regulates our lives and allows us to live together with the minimum of tension in mass-societies, this would only a feature to be recommended if mass-societies could be shown to be an unmitigated good. In the absence of such proof it becomes simply a feature of our society, just as a communal military upbringing was a feature of Spartan society in the Classical Greek period.

Moreover, as viewers of the BBC television series *Yes Minister* will know, the function of bureaucracies is not to process the edicts of government, but to make sure as little change as possible takes place. And this again is simply a feature of modernity, not a point of criticism since if, as can be easily demonstrated, in any society a majority of people are incompetent, both in personal and public life, then structures to ensure that a minimum of change takes place are a *desideratum*. The question arises, however, as to how the bureaucratic structures of modernity will be able to cope with sudden catastrophic changes of the sort that are likely to occur with greater frequency in the future. The answer is probably very badly, since in previous national emergencies, such as the Second World War, the bureaucracies coped by switching to their putative role of edict-processors and being supplemented by independent think-tanks, yet emergencies in the future, of the ecological kind, will not require more heroic increases in production and technological derring-do of the sort which occurred during the Second World War, but an orderly scaling-back of modernity's activities. This is something that modernity has never encountered before and for which its bureaucracies, as currently constituted, will be utterly incompetent.

6. Finally one illusion we should take care to divest ourselves of is that somehow our society is better able to face up to its problems and find solutions to them because it is democratic. Readers of my chapter two will have noted how little my account figured any influence from the democratic process on the course of modernity (§4.7).

Besides this democratic politics as exercised in developed countries consists of constructing coalitions of between 30-50% of the voters (this process is very clear in countries where proportional representation is in force). This bloc, whether it belongs to right- or left-of-centre parties is effectively the voice of the high bourgeoisie, and proceeds to enact all the policies which maintain and foster the economic conditions which perpetuate its hold on power (was there ever a political bloc which, knowingly, connived at its own downfall?). The rest of the voters are either too apathetic, or too down-trodden to care, as witness the incredibly low voter turn-out figures in the US and the UK. Even countries where voting is compulsory, we might suspect, have the same tendency, since there voters who would ordinarily have not voted simply vote unthinkingly for the party their parent's voted for, or their spouse tells them to vote for.

Moreover, as we have seen, 'democracy' has become simply the standard euphemism for the safeguarding of western interests (§7.4.4).

6. Furthermore, despite our plethora of news and information services we are not well-served by our media (§7.4.4), which finds the complexities of the real world difficult to get over in a way which will 'sell' the paper or the TV channel. Even on quite reputable TV channels it is frequently necessary to already know the background to a story to interpret a news report, anyone not in possession of such knowledge is left floundering with lurid pictures and a breathless commentary, signifying nothing. And most media are now not even trying to convey information, but, backed up by sophisticated audience research, pander to the very worse prejudices of their reviewers or readers in the interests of ratings and more advertising revenue; as Chomsky brilliantly put it: 'The advertisers are the clients, the readers [or viewers] are the product'.

In the world of publishing the story is the same – nothing remotely threatening to modernity can ever get published; the nearest approach to such works would be those of authors such as Noam Chomsky or Germaine Greer, who are too notorious to ignore. Careful academic works are very useful, but have to be interpreted to reinsert the anti-modernistic moral which the self-censorship of the writer has elided. Another unfortunate aspect of publishing is the way in which works are increasingly being made to conform rigidly with the arbitrary boundaries of the academic disciplines and confine their scope to single issues.There has recently, for example, been much published on separate environmental issues, as though pollution, nuclear weapons, loss of ecological resources were not all part of the one problem.

7. A final note to add in this section is that we can expect still less to find opposition in the developing world. This is because spaces for opposition are more limited there. Moreover if the usual fate of an environmental activist in the developed world is to be ignored, the fate of his/her colleague in the developing world is usually to be silenced, one way or another. Because the developing world

is disadvantaged *vis à vis* the developed world, opposition there is more profound, but likely to be less politically developed and more prone to be violently extirpated.

8.3 In other words we cannot expect any sort of wide-spread opposition to modernity to emerge, spontaneously or not, from 'the people'. But perhaps this is not surprising, and to expect that opposition might so arise is a hang-over from the Romantic/liberal notion that, if only enough consciences are raised, then the thing is effectively done; this is based on the idea that the citizens of society are currently deluded by ideology, but will, in the fullness of time emerge into a bright, and unideological future. This is impossible, for the citizenry, far from being deluded by ideology, *are* the ideology. Nor can anyone be free from ideology (or a set of cultural presuppositions); all we can hope for is the future emergence of an ideology which produce a better outcomes.

Furthermore what this view ignores is firstly that it is very difficult to persuade people to come to a disinterested view of their own interests, as opposed to a sort of theoretical acknowledgment that everything isn't quite as well-ordered as it might be, and secondly, that even if this view is elicited then the actual process of changing institutions and political processes is still to be accomplished. We are governed not so much by our opinions, attitudes and ideology, but by our institutions. Institutions are historical artefacts like everything else and are susceptible to change. That institutions function currently as Ideological State Apparatus, (in the Althusserian phrase), does not invalidate their future, praeter-modern uses, but they are, perhaps of all things, the most resistant to change.

Yet it is to the institutional parts of modernity that we should look for the changes that will be necessary for any move to a praeter-modern society. As against one of the arguments of, for example F.E.Trainer in his *Abandon Affluence*, we should be wary of assuming that the praeter-modern world will be an anarchistic and utopian one (269). Human beings, especially modern ones recently deprived of their living-standards, are very dangerous creatures and it seems obvious that any dismantling of modernity would need to be rigorously policed until humans had lost the habit of thinking capitalistically. In any case there is a fair argument to be made that modernity itself is already a state of anarchy and no more 'liberation of desire', of the sort envisaged by over-excitable French Marxists like Deleuze and Guattari, is either necessary or desirable.

Those of us who wish to see an end to modernity should not neglect consciousness-raising, or the organisation of workers (or non-workers), but this must form part of a very well thought-out campaign, waged in all countries to capture and change the institutions of governmental regulation, political life, international politics (the UN), as well as the various NGOs, professional and business organisations. Quite how this campaign should be organised, who should lead it, how it should go about its activities, and how it should put its platform across, is difficult to imagine. However I believe that such a broad-fronted coalition is the only way to make any progress towards modifying the course of modernity.

A final point to make in this section is that the traditional argument against coalition politics, 'the politics of special interest groups' as it is often called is that the goals of such politics end up by being so diluted by the necessary compromises that have to have been made, that its achievements are hardly worth the efforts that went into formulating the goals in the first place. We should bear this in mind as a consideration for future discussion.

8.4 Finally then we can begin to discuss what the policies that might be able to bring about an orderly end to modernity might look like. It seems to me that there are four things to bear in mind here.

1. Any oppositional politics must recognise that the owners of capital are the holders of political power (Birrell 1). Although there are precedents for neglecting business-interests, and even expropriating capital in national emergencies, yet the sort of fundamental change which is proposed here, a planned change in advance of any external imperative to change, will need the cooperation and the finance of the business-sector. Consequently any change that is proposed must give the impression of being in the business-sector's immediate interests.

2. That as the middle-class (God bless 'em) are such a powerful force for conservatism, any proposed change must similarly not give the impression that it will dramatically alter the living-standards and the life-styles of the middle-classes.

3. That as (§8.3) the coalition that must be engaged to try to bring about change will be so broad and multifarious then the goals of the coalition must be as limited as possible. That is, the goal of trying to bring an orderly end to modernity must not be confused with the search for justice, the search for peace, for women's rights &c. I am assuming that these searches might be easier in a praeter-modern world, but this is just an assumption. The fewer things which surface to distract the political process of seeking an end to modernity, the more likely it will be to succeed.

4. However, this campaign should have the object of bringing about a series of radical changes that would mean the end of global capitalism and hence modernity, and should not be reluctant to put this goal forward as its *raison d'être*.

Chapter Nine:
The Future

9.1 In §8.4 I laid out the criteria that a political solution to the problems of modernity must fulfil if it is to have any chance of success. Now I can lay out what I think is a reasonable and attainable solution, which logically follows from what I have said about the nature of modernity and the way it maintains its predominance.

The first stage therefore would be a return to the international conditions of middle capitalism, viz fixed exchange rates. This will be quite a popular move, as most countries have had their fingers burnt by the vagaries of the international market in currencies. But this in itself is not enough, we have already seen that even a moderately-regulated international market is still based on international exploitation and the need for growth (§2.5). Even the much-vaunted Swedish welfare-state only brought a high-standard of living at a price, namely high energy consumption (Birrell 3).

What needs to occur is for the regulation of international trading to continue on a well-planned and logical path so that, year by year, more and more commodity prices are fixed, more and more impediments are put in the way of international trade. By the end of the process, in the medium term (30-50 years) the world should consist of a number of independent states (who may or may not have ceded most of their external powers to the UN), but who are largely economically self-sufficient and do not to any great extent rely upon foreign trade, either for basics, or for wealth-creation.

How well this scheme is received depends on how well it is presented, since it ultimately promises the best deal for everyone in the long term. Moreover there are ample precedents for the banning of trade in certain items, such as drugs, and most countries have very well-organised customs services, which would be able to engage in policing these restrictions. Restrictions on trade could begin with commodities in very short supply, such as tropical hardwoods, and things of

MAGDALEN COLLEGE LIBRARY

obvious inutility, such as weapons. The recent dismantling of many of Iraq's 'weapons of mass-destruction' is a very heartening precedent for this idea, but there is no reason why such a course of action need be confined to Iraq; it would seem to be a very sensible solution to be applied to the US, Russia, Britain, France, China, in fact any country possessing excessive offensive capability.

Note also how this solution fulfils the criteria listed in §8.4 as requirements of a solution. Firstly it strikes fundamentally at the heart of modernity, turning back its global reach and restricting its search for newer and yet newer markets (§8.4.4). However it will certainly, so long as it is formulated and implemented carefully, not cause the short-term profits of companies to suffer, as many new markets, formerly occupied by foreign companies and products will open up (§8.4.1). This would apply to developing countries too. Again, because of the nature of the changes taking place, middle-class incomes in developed countries would not suffer, instead there would be greatly increased demand for lawyers, accountants, administrators and other professionals (§8.4.2). Finally, these changes represent an administrative rather than a spiritual change and, because of their very practical and mundane nature, cannot be seen as being involved with any other political or social cause, and therefore opposed for that reason (§8.4.3).

9.2 As this scenario is open to misinterpretation from a number of directions I should like to try to anticipate as many of these in this section.
1. The solution I have offered is not one grand solution, not one magic blueprint *à la* Plato, or *à la* Marx, or, for that matter *à la* international capitalism, but a suggestion for a political process. Nor is it one identical solution to be applied everywhere, it is simply a way of establishing the pre-conditions for any future solutions to environmental problems. The world is brimming with ingenious green solutions to environmental problems, but without a political paradigm or paradigms in which to try them out they never will be tried out. What this solution offers is the chance for a diversity of political and cultural units of the world to find their own solutions; as the ecological problems of modernity are so grave then none of the solutions that will be necessary will be either easy or simple, though the environment for them to be thought through will be created.

Nor is it a sort of plea for cultural essentialism. I have, throughout this work, repeatedly laid down that cultures are not essential, timeless artefacts, but constructions in time from diverse and contingent elements. There is no greater intellectual pleasure than considering the hybridity of cultures; but in a situation where one culture (that of modernity) seems able effortlessly to absorb all cultural difference within itself and subvert every other culture in its quest for growth and markets, then reluctantly it is necessary to contemplate as a solution an artificial segregation of cultures by means of restrictions on trade and, therefore, travel.

2. This is not an autarchic/autarkic solution for the sake of autarchy/autarkic, as practised by such regimes as Ceasescu's Roumania or (until recently) by the current regime in Burma. These regimes were and are (respectively) very unpleasant. But they would probably be unpleasant even if they had traded internationally. There are also very many very nasty regimes who do trade internationally. We shouldn't ever confuse openness, in the sense of the flow of ideas and information with the flows of the international market. We have seen how the international media, whilst trying to convey information simply conveys a western view of the world (§7.4.4). Its major function at present seems to be to supply information of the less-developed world's wants to itself. As Dr Johnson observed in another recently-colonised society (the Scottish Highlands in the 1770s): 'Their [the Highlanders'] ignorance grows everyday less, but their knowledge is yet of little use other than to show them their wants.'

Similarly the trade in technology means that technology is not a solution to problems, but a source of political control and oppression. One reform which would be a great help in the praeter-modern world would be the ending of the copyright on ideas, 'intellectual property' — this copyright has never served to protect inventors and has only ever resulted in large companies getting very rich by charging large sums for the use of simple ideas.

To return to Roumania and Burma; these regimes deliberately cut themselves off from the world. We have seen how any such change in modernity must be global, otherwise the individual countries will be penalised (§6.2). Thus if all the countries of the world are cutting off their external trade no one country will be penalised. It is also to be hoped that individual countries manage themselves with a better regard for social justice and more competently than Roumania and Burma.

3. There is a widespread idea that without the 'international policeman' of 'democratic capitalism' the world would fall apart, but this is so laughably patronising and racist as to be not worth contradicting. In any case I am not suggesting that the world would be a sort of bear-pit of squabbling countries, but under the aegis of United Nations, which would have assumed many of the external functions of the various countries, though not trade.

Furthermore it is to be observed that much of the nastiness of the world comes from elites making sure that their citizens are quiescent to their capitalistic system, or from richer economies oppressing poorer ones. This scheme is designed to take away this very motive, and should allow most countries and cultures to return to far less frenzied, and more traditional, power-games.

Finally it should be observed that all the really lawless places in the world, such as parts of Papua New Guinea, cities in the Third World and the US, are so because their populations consist of many different groups of people brought

MAGDALEN COLLEGE LIBRARY

suddenly together, with extremes of wealth and poverty. In such situations the traditional cultural mechanisms which control violence are lost sight of and the various groups battle it out, making one another scapegoats for their own poverty and oppression. A praeter-modern world organised on the lines I am suggesting should allow greater scope for more even-handed and reasonable settlements to be made in such warring societies.

4. It may be the case that, as a result of this schema, disruption and a drop in living standards will occur in the less developed world, particularly in the over-stretched cities. However it is to be hoped that the developed world will still continue its aid-programmes and technological and logistic support to the less developed world. I don't think that the more developed world will suffer in the short-term, as the 'autarkic kick' spurs on economies (this will apply to the less developed world as well). Ultimately, of course the wished-for outcome of these proposals *is* a drop in living-standards, *as currently measured*, for the developed world, since the standard of living which obtains at the moment is ecologically unsustainable.

This proposal represents a sensible way of maximising capital, thus the developed world will be largely restricted to the capital gained in the last 200 years of economic development, and the less-developed world to the still-existing natural capital inhering in its natural resources. Thus when I agreed with Dr Mohathir that the West should pay to preserve the environment in countries like Malaysia (§7.5), I was thinking of this in terms of the West's foregoing its consumption of tropical hardwoods and therefore leaving the use of the forests to the people of the area in which they grow. This is course will be no comfort to the westernised comprador class that the good doctor belongs to, since the only use for the forests will then be small-scale local exploitation and the traditional uses of indigenous peoples.

As to the possible charge that nations will not have the goods they need, this is very unlikely since rarely in pre-modern times was a society completely dependent for some necessity on material from outside its own territory. But obviously if it were found that there was some country in this unfortunate predicament, then trade in that commodity should be allowed to continue.

A final benefit of this proposal is that it would reunite the processes of production and consumption, which have been almost wholly detached by modernity (Chrisholm in Turner, 97). This would result in greater accountability of the producers, and greater efficiency all round.

5. In this scheme the UN would still exist and can become more of a forum for the adjudication of complaints against various regimes. But, as pointed out in point 3 above, the praeter-modern world will not need rely to such a great extent on violence as a political tool and therefore 'human rights' (of whatever sort, by whatever definition) should be better respected.

The whole point of these proposals will be to lift the pressure on the environment; much environmental protection currently follows the western dichotomy of 'cultivated land/wilderness' which has no basis in reality (§6.12). These proposals should allow states and nations to think through more imaginative protection for special areas (though all areas are special really); protection which would not simply lock them away, but allow human use and interaction with them, recognising that ecosystems only have meaning when mediated through human use of them.

It is almost inevitable that countries, developed or not developed will try to cheat, and use ecologically-damaging technology to prop up standards of living. Here (since environmental degradation knows no boundaries) an efficient international environmental protection agency with strong powers is clearly a necessity. In the modern world nations and cultures have every freedom but that of not participating in the world economy, that is, no freedom at all. In the praeter-modern world it is to be hoped that cultures will have every freedom but the freedom to go down the capitalist road again, that is, every freedom bar one.

6. As to the idea that trading is some sort of basic human right I would reply that trading is a basic human *activity*, and one which no culture is wholly ignorant of. But we must not confuse trade with international capitalism, which is just a form of economic plunder and imperialism. The trading which took place in Aboriginal Australia, for example, was concerned with information, technology, ritual objects, and plants and material not found in the receiving group's territory. However trading, though useful, was not vital to any group and was even-handed, a reciprocal arrangement that did not imply the predominance or superiority of either party. This is what international trade has entailed for one group of Aborigines since western settlement:

> I saw the bulldozers rip through our Gumatj country. Bauxite mining doesn't just mean digging a hole in the ground—that would be bad enough. It means bulldozing the land, many square kilometres, scraping off the surface. I watched my father as he stood in front of bulldozers to stop them clearing the sacred trees, and chase away bulldozer drivers with an axe. I watched him crying when our sacred waterhole, which was one of our dreamings *and a source of water*, was bulldozed. (Yunupingu, 46-47, my italics)

Finally we should note that we are not trying to stop trade itself, but international trade. Obviously various modes of exchange will still obtain in the national economies I envisage.

7. Regrettable as it is, modern nation-states are what we have to deal with. It is to be hoped that such monstrosities as the United States, Brazil, Russia, China &c &c

will quickly collapse and be replaced by a number of smaller political units, and if, over time, local economies might spring up in what might be called 'eco-regions', then so much the better. But understand, the provisions outlined in the chapter are not for the purpose of creating a sort of Taoist state of affairs, where everyone remains in the places where he/she was born, and the inhabitants of neighbouring villages rarely meet each other. What should emerge is what characterised the pre-modern world, namely a number of economies, all involving trade of various kinds. If the US, Brazil &c want to carry on a sort of suicidal modernistic growth, then they can — all that will have changed is that they will not (because of the international treaties and safeguards) be able to expand their activities outside their borders, and involve everyone else in their imprudence. They would not, as they are allowed to do at the moment, contravene the legal maxim of *sic utere tuo ut alienum non laedas* ('One should use his property in such a way as to avoid injury to that of another') (Wilder 5).

This proposal is best thought of as permitting the setting up of various experimental economies; it differs from modernity in that everyone is not caught up in the same mad experiment.

8. The difficulty of policing such and arrangement need not be overestimated — everything that is policed is difficult to police, otherwise there would be no need to police it. At the moment there are more administrators, accountants, lawyers, bureaucrats, than at any time in history — if we can't run this then we need a new science of administration.

International crime will represent a major threat to the success of this proposal, especially in the early stages. However, restrictions on international banking, travel and communications will make life more difficult for criminals, for international crime is just a parody of international Free Trade. Recently I saw a headline asking 'Can Colombia Conquer Drugs?', which should surely have read 'Can the USA Conquer Drugs?'; like international trade, international crime exports the blame for modernity's excesses from the guilty to the innocent. Besides this the details of how to combat such threats, as well as all the details of this proposal, are such as need to be thought through at greater length and in greater detail than is possible here.

9. I admit that the most serious objection to this proposal, is that it could never get off the ground. I have already discussed the difficulty of bringing together a coalition for this purpose in the developed world (§8.4) and have, beyond noting the difficulty, nothing further to add.

It is not true that nations have never given up their sovereign powers and I believe that after the next depression in the world economy (which will probably occur c.1997-2000), there will be many countries desperate to shelter behind internationally regulated trade. Whether *all* countries, or enough to force the others, will want to is a different matter, it is to be hoped that it will not take another battering from the next recession to push countries into agreement. Yet how to persuade the international community to go further into the sort of far-reaching changes that I have proposed is a different matter again.

10. A final point which I should like to restate is that these proposals are not designed to remove perennial human vices; under any sort of future polity cruelty, greed, stupidity and short-sightedness would remain, because these are part of the genetic and cultural makeup of all humans, all that this scenario envisages is that these vices will no longer be magnified and argued for as a good. They will still be present, but as side-issues, not as the basis of polity.

9.3 Thinking about the sorts of changes that might be necessary in the praeter-modern world I am struck by the thought that we in the developed countries are, strangely enough, much less well equipped to deal with them than are the people of the less developed world. This is because most of the peoples of the less developed world are well used to the sort of hardships that will be entailed. But another reason is that they, to put it bluntly, are not involved in modernity's great drama, as we are. It has been fascinating to follow events in the former Soviet Union and to see that almost as bad as the fall in living standards has been the loss of face of the people, finding that their country has turned in a couple of years from a superpower to a second-rate nation. In the west any change to praeter-modernity will be a similar loss of pride as well as a loss of economic predominance. It will therefore be necessary to find in the resources of our own and possibly other cultures some abiding myths to replace those of human progress, economic development *et cetera*.

I should like to adumbrate two. The first is that of even-handed, almost ritual, Aboriginal Australian trade that we have already mentioned (§9.2.6). This can stand as a metaphor for pre-modern trade, something that may indeed have created wealth, but which was peripheral to the main activity of society. The other is more difficult to grasp. Consider the well-known graph of world-population. For all of recorded history it has been rising very gradually, despite local fluctuations. In about 1850 it suddenly takes off, as I have argued because of the global cultural space created by modernity (§6.8). However, suppose that this had not occurred; if we extrapolate the line of population growth we would arrive at the population figure for the present of rather less than 1 billion people.

Imagine as well all the other statistics of technological and economic growth, how they might have appeared if instead of the sudden leap into the stratosphere of the nineteenth and twentieth centuries, they too had carried on the same quiet growth. It seems to me that what has been wrong with modernistic and capitalistic growth is that it has been too sudden; seven generations are all that have elapsed since the beginnings of modernity. Three long and overlapping life-times (say 1800-1880, 1870-1940, 1930-present) are all that have supervened between us in the west and pre-modern times. This is surely too fast for any social and economic order to cope with and indeed the present world-order seems amply to confirm this fact.

But although modernity's economic development has been a failure, yet there is always the underlying quiet amelioration of conditions, development of resources and natural systems, which is a consequence simply of humanity's continued residence on the planet. I call this 'invisible growth'; this is the growth that modernity, in its fantastic dash towards disaster, cannot see, but it is the sort of human activity which has always gone on, as other great civilisations, trial-runs for modernity, have risen and crashed about it. It is this sort of growth that will continue long after modernity's achievements have been deservedly forgotten.

9.4 I should not, however, like to end on such a hopeful note. For I do not believe that it is likely that a solution to the problems caused by modernity, like that which I have just outlined, or some other scheme, will in fact be able to be implemented, for two reasons. The first is that the delusion that technology and further economic growth can solve the problems that were caused by technology and economic growth will undoubtedly persist, such is their prestige, until the very last moment. This will prevent the re-interpretion of elements within western (or Confucian) culture in a more useful sense until it is too late to do so in a quiet, orderly manner. The second is that modernity so overshadows any other cultures that elements from them cannot be imported into modernity to fulfil the need we have of, for example, some concept of limits, or a better model of the functionings of humans and nature, or, as I argued earlier, humans-in-nature and nature-with-humans.

I think that something like what I call praeter-modernity will come into being anyway, some time within the next few centuries, for there is every precedent in history for this outcome: whenever any overextended political paradigm collapses it has produced a return to local governments and economies; indeed I would argue that these periods, those which historians label 'dark ages' or 'periods of disunity' are the more normal state of affairs, and it is the so-called great civilisations, with their military might and centralised governments which are the problem in the first place.

However it would be much more preferable if such a state of affairs were to come into being as a part of a planned end to modernity. For if modernity collapses, perhaps early next century, perhaps centuries hence, it may be remembered, not as a political paradigm which deserved to fail, but as a sort of a mythological Golden Age of Peace (!) and Plenty. A parallel might be with China (and here I am talking about China proper, viz the Huang-Ho and Yangtze river valleys, not the extended empire that the People's Republic now controls). Here, for the majority of its history, Chinese culture or cultures has/have been fragmented, politically organised in various states, or statelets. Nevertheless there is an abiding myth of the unified Chinese State, which has caused more wars and misery, as each small state sees it as its destiny to win overall control, than the small-scale squabbles of less ambitions and less deluded rulers would ever have done. Similarly, in the case of praeter-modernity, there would then be the desire to try to resurrect modernity in one guise or another, and world history would probably continue in a boom and bust cycle for centuries, as huge and wasteful efforts were made to return to an overbearing and wasteful paradigm. What is needed is for a symbolic disowning of modernity, before it comes to an end of its own accord.

So much, then, for these things.

Bibliography

Avineri, Shlomo, ed and intro. *Karl Marx on Colonialism and Modernisation: His Dispatches and Other Writings on China, India, Mexico, the Middle East and North Africa.* New York: Doubleday, 1968.

Beaud, Michel. *A History of Capitalism 1500-1980.* Trans Tom Dickinson and Anny Lefebvre. London: Macmillan Press, 1984.

Beder, Sharon. *The Nature of Sustainable Development.* Newham, Victoria: Scribe, 1993.

Bellett, A.J.D. *The Evolution of Societal Values Compatible with Ecological Sustainability.* Canberra: Australian National University Centre for Resource and Environmental Studies, 1990.

Bettinger, Robert. *Hunter Gatherers: Archaeological and Evolutionary Theory.* New York: Plenum Press, 1991.

Birrell, Robert. *From Growth to Sustainability: Implications of the Swedish Experience.* Canberra: Australian National University Centre for Resource and Environmental Studies, 1990.

Cline, William R. *The Economics of Global Warming.* Washington DC: Institute for International Economics, 1992.

Crosby, Alfred. *Biological Imperialism: The Ecological Expansion of Europe 900-1900.* Cambridge: Cambridge University Press, 1986.

Handmer, John. 'Sustainability, Vulnerability and Disaster'. *Social Structures for Sustainability.* Ed Peter Cock. Canberra: Australian National University Centre for Resource and Environmental Studies, 1991: 73-9.

Holmes, Sandra Le Brun. *Yirawala: Painter of the Dreaming.* Sydney: Hale and Iremonger, 1994.

Howe, K.R *et al*, eds. *Tides of History: The Pacific Islands in the Twentieth Century.* Sydney: Allen and Unwin, 1994.

Illich, Ivan. *Shadow Work.* Boston: Boyars, 1981.

Jacobs, Michael. *The Green Economy: Environment, Sustainable Development and the Politics of the Future.* London: Pluto Press, 1991.

Kaniff, S. 'Renewable Energy'. *Energy Options for Sustainability.* Ed Stephen Dovers. Canberra: Australian National University Centre for Resource and Environmental Studies, 1991: 48-100.

Keynes, John Maynard. 'The Economic Possibilities for Our Grandchildren' (1930). *Essays in Persuasion*. London: Macmillan, 1931: 358-73.

Lee, Martyn J. *Consumer Culture Reborn: The Cultural Politics of Consumption*. London: Routledge, 1993.

McKeown, Thomas. *The Origins of Human Disease*. Oxford: Blackwell, 1988.

Marx, Karl. *Capital* (ie *Das Kapital*) (1867). Chicago: Encyclopedia Britannica Inc, 1952.

— — and Friedrich Engels. 'Manifesto of the Communist Party' (1848). *Capital*. Chicago: Encyclopedia Britannica Inc, 1952: 413-34.

— —. *Pre-Capitalist Economic Formations*. Ed E.J.Hobsbawm. London: Lawrence and Wishart, 1964.

Mokyr, Joel, Ed. The British Industrial Revolution: An Economic Perspective. Boulder, Col: Westview Press, 1993.

Pearce, Fred. 'Acid Rain'. *New Scientist* 5th November 1987.

Rackham, Oliver. *The History of the Countryside*. London: Dent, 1986.

Robinson, Joan. *Selected Economic Writings*. Bombay: Oxford University Press, 1974.

Rose, Margaret A. *The Post-Modern and the Post-Industrial: A Critical Analysis*. Cambridge: Cambridge University Press, 1991.

Smith, Adam. *An Inquiry into the Nature and Causes of the Wealth of Nations* (1776). Ed Edward Cannan. Chicago: U of Chicago Press, 1976.

Thoughton, J.T et al. *Climatic Change 1992: The Supplementary Report to the IPCC Scientific Assessment*. Cambridge: Cambridge University Press, 1992.

Trainer, F.E. *Abandon Affluence!* London: Zed Books, 1985.

Turner, B.L II et al, eds. *The Earth as Transformed by Human Action: Global and Regional Changes in the Biosphere Over the Past 300 Years*. Cambridge: Cambridge University Press, 1990.

Weber, Max. *The Protestant Ethic and the Spirit of Capitalism* (1920). Ed Talcott Parsons. London: Unwin University Books, 1930.

Wilder, Martijn. *Liability on Ice: Environmental Damage and the Antarctic Madrid Protocol*. Canberra: Australian National University Centre for Resource and Environmental Studies, 1993.

White, Deborah. 'On Stony Ground and Among Thistles'. *Social Structures for Sustainability*. Ed Peter Cock. Canberra: Australian National University Centre for Resource and Environmental Studies, 1991: 52-62.

World Resources Institute. *World Resources 1994-95: A Guide to the World Environment*. New York: Oxford University Press, 1994.

Yunupingu, Galarrwuy. 'What I See'. *Republica No.1*. Sydney: Augus and Roberston, 1994: 46-47.

Ziman, John. *Reliable Knowledge: An Exploration of the Grounds for Belief in Science*. Cambridge: Cambridge University Press, 1973.

Index